Fishing in Derbyshire and Around

Gallichan, Walter M. (Walter Matthew)

BIBLIOLIFE

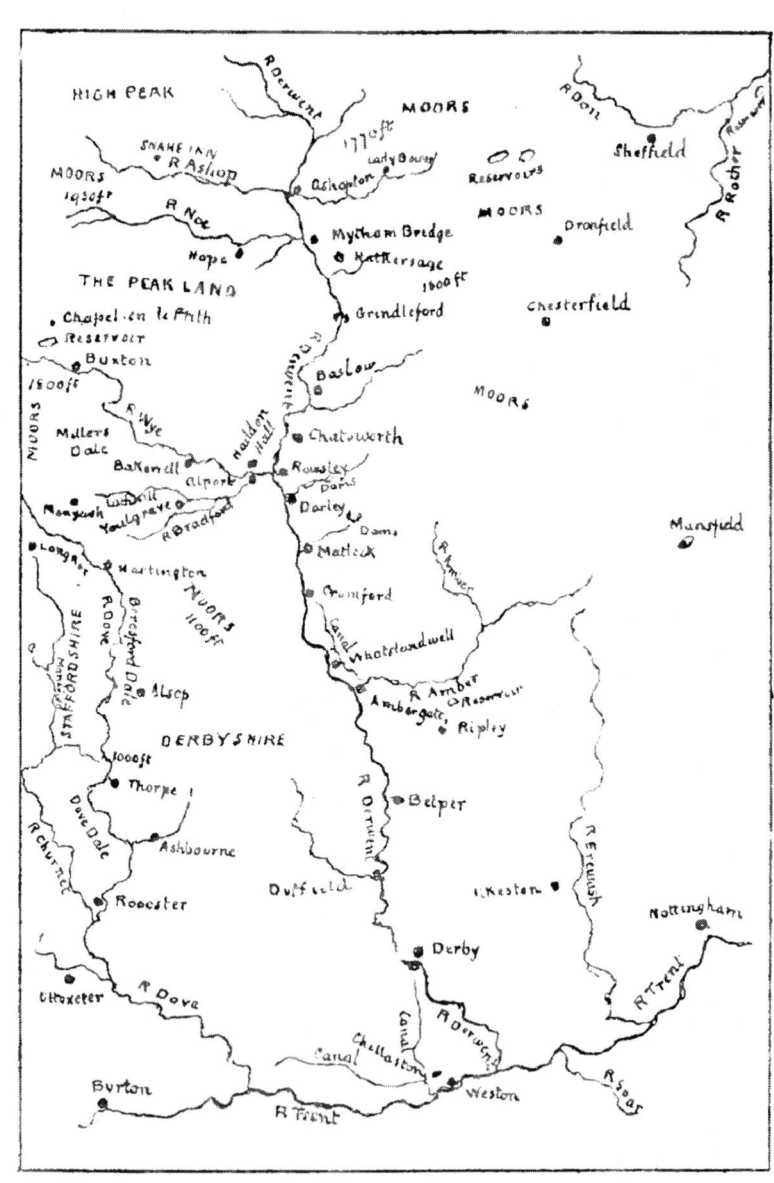

FISHING MAP OF WATERS.

(DRAWN BY W. M. G.)

FISHING IN DERBYSHIRE
AND AROUND

BY

WALTER M. GALLICHAN

('GEOFFREY MORTIMER')

AUTHOR OF 'FISHING IN WALES'

LONDON

F. E. ROBINSON & CO.

20 GREAT RUSSELL STREET

1905

TO

MY FRIEND

DOCTOR SIDNEY HILLIER

(*Stowmarket*)

AN ENTHUSIASTIC FLY-FISHERMAN

THIS BOOK IS DEDICATED

PREFACE

SOME years ago I used to find myself inquiring, in the 'ever-returning spring,' 'Where shall I go to fish ?' In those days there were but few books for anglers containing directions as to the finding of fishing waters, and descriptions of the streams in a stated district. For example, one might have read diligently all that had then been written upon the Derbyshire Derwent or Wye without learning whether those rivers were open or private fisheries, where one could stay upon their banks, and how much a fishing holiday would cost. There are a number of fishermen still in this plight. How many of us have travelled more than once to a far corner of the kingdom, with mingled expect_ ancy and misgiving, to fish in a river about which we have been able to gather little or nothing in the way of practical information! Such expeditions, as I know from experience, frequently end in disillusionment and waste of time.

The gratifying assurances of fishermen that my ' Fishing in Wales ' has proved acceptable and useful, and the generous commendation accorded to that book by reviewers, have encouraged me while writing the present volume. Perhaps I may here say that the collection and arranging of material for such a book is not unaccompanied by peculiar difficulties. My aim is to strike the happy mean betwixt overstatement of the sport that may be expected in a given stream and the peril of a pessimistic view.

There is an old-standing accusation against anglers that they are, to express it politely, prone to extravagance of statement. It matters not if the fishing writer is by nature severely dispassionate and impartial. He will not escape the charge, let it be facetious or spiteful. Someone will tell him that he has drawn the long-bow. In order to guard against inaccuracy, I have not remained satisfied with relating my own experience of rivers in this district. My personal investigation has been supplemented by many interviews and a considerable correspondence with the secretaries and members of fishing societies, riparian owners, and water-bailiffs Probably I have erred now and then on the side of cautiousness. If so, I may be pardoned for a shrinking from that not altogether kindly banter to which anglers are exposed. At any rate, I may state that I have been at much trouble to impart trustworthy information.

I hope that there is no omission of any of the names of those friends and correspondents who have assisted me in writing this book. My thanks for obligations are due to Mr. A. P. Payne-Gallwey, to Sir Thomas Wardle, to Mr. T. C. Jeffrey, of the Midland Railway Company, to Dr. S. Warneford, to Mr. W. H. Foster, of Ashbourne, and to several fishermen whose names will be found in the text. From out of the large number of authorities from whom I sought knowledge only two ignored my request. To these I accord my free absolution. The interest shown in my project convinces me that the great majority of resident Derbyshire anglers welcome viators in the cheery and fraternal spirit of Izaak Walton.

WALTER M. GALLICHAN.

THE CRIMBLES,
    YOULGREAVE, BAKEWELL,
        DERBYSHIRE,
March, 1905.

CONTENTS

Contents

FISHING IN DERBYSHIRE AND AROUND

CHAPTER I

A GENERAL CHAPTER

IT is scarcely necessary to extol the attractions of rivers rendered classic by association with the names of Izaak Walton and Charles Cotton. The pleasant task that I have set myself is to direct the fisherman to the streams and angling waters of a beautiful district, comprising the county of Derbyshire and some parts of the adjoining shires. Other writers, in the past, have described the rivers of this region from the point of view of the tourist in search of the picturesque ; while, here and there, amongst angling volumes that are out of print, one finds a few accounts of Walton and the Dove, and an occasional reference to the Derwent, Wye, and other trout-streams.

During the past thirty or forty years, one or

I

two interesting books have been added to the scant collection of angling literature appertaining generally to the Midlands. The veteran who writes so charmingly under the name of ' The Amateur Angler ' has given us his impressions of Dovedale, and in his book on ' The Trout,' the Marquess of Granby has told us of enticing sport by his own lengths of the Lathkill and Bradford.

When I chose Derbyshire for my home, after some years of wandering, it was suggested to me that I should endeavour to set forth the claims of that county upon the angler, in the same way that I have described sport with the rod in Wales and Spain. Falling in with the hint, I sit down to-day, with the song of a trout-stream in the dale below borne across the garden, to begin the survey of familiar stretches of rivers endeared to me, and to lead the brother of the angle to runs and pools where he may cast his ' Derbyshire bumble ' in the wet style of fly-fishing, or stalk the well-proportioned trout in translucent water, and drop his dry fly in the dimple of a rise. Nor shall I forget to disclose to the bottom-fisher the exact points where he may expect to find pike, roach, chub, barbel, grayling, and other fish in the proper seasons.

Nature has provided kindly for both the fly-fisher and bottom-fisherman in this district. Most of the large and small tributaries of the Trent contain chiefly trout and grayling in their higher waters. Where the game fish are scarce in these rivers—that is to say, in their lower lengths—coarse fish are in some instances very abundant. This is a most excellent provision, for reaches that harbour chub, perch, and pike can be avoided by the fly-fisherman.

In another respect the rivers in Derbyshire and around claim the attention of visiting anglers. The means of communication from the chief towns of the North and South, and within the district itself, enable the visitor to reach the riverside within a few hours. For instance, fishermen residing in Manchester and its surrounding towns, or in Derby and Nottingham, can leave home at a reasonable hour in the morning, spend a day by the Derwent or Dove, and return by an evening train. The quick service of trains on the Midland Railway enables the fisherman to travel by a fast morning train from St. Pancras to Matlock or Bakewell, in plenty of time for an afternoon and evening with the trout and grayling of the Derwent and Wye;

while week-end tickets on this line, at reduced fares, are issued to all the chief fishing stations. The district under our consideration is, therefore, easily accessible, and compares very favourably in this matter with Wales or the West of England.

As to the cost of fishing, and board and lodging, I shall refer to the charges in describing the various rivers and the towns and villages upon their banks. Some of the fishing lengths in private hands can be fished by permission of the land-owners or tenants holding rights of angling, and portions of the rivers are fishable by taking quarters at comfortable hotels. There are also preserved waters, which are controlled by associations, and daily, weekly, and season tickets can be purchased at a moderate cost. The Conservators of the Trent issue licenses to fish with rod and line for trout and char in the main river and its tributaries at half a crown for the season, and one shilling for one week. This license covers almost the whole of the rivers mentioned in these pages.

The streams of Derbyshire and the bordering counties offer considerable diversity both in the character of their scenery and their waters. In the limestone regions watered by the Dove, the Wye, the Lathkill, the Manifold, and the middle lengths of the Derwent, the streams are normally clear, and have the transparent quality of the Hampshire rivers and the chalk streams of Berks and Bucks. The Lathkill has water of remarkable limpidity, and almost the same may be said for the Wye during dry weather. In the Dove the angler will find a very slight colour, but it is still, in its reaches from the source to the lower end of Dovedale, a bright stream, with scarcely a perceptible stain in a fine summer.

Surface water soon colours these rivers, but fairly heavy rain is required to render them turbid for some days together, and I have seen the upper Lathkill quite clear when the stream had over-flown its banks at several points. A brown stain in the Wye is an advantage, but occasionally during rainy seasons the stream is much swollen, and the water remains muddy for a few days.

The Derwent takes a tint from the peat in its upper waters, and after rain it is tinged with 'woodland water' from the woods that clothe its banks above Chatsworth. Under ordinary summer conditions this river is not so limpid as its tributary the Wye, and from Matlock downwards it is discoloured with drainage for some distance, to assume a clearer character in the swift shallows of Cromford and Whatstandwell. Lower down, in the neighbourhood of Ambergate and Belper, the Derwent is less impetuous, and its water is somewhat deeply coloured throughout the rest of its course to the Trent.

The trout and grayling rivers of Derbyshire differ in certain essential characteristics from the rushing, boulder-strewn streams of North Wales and the Scottish Highlands. Limestone determines their clearness, and the springs whence some of them arise are among rocky uplands. We may perhaps say that the trout-streams of the High Peak Country are far wilder than those of the South of England, but not so wild generally as the rivers of Scotland and Wales. They possess an intermediate character, with certain resemblances to the clear southern streams and the boisterous, peat-stained rivers of the North. Picturesque is the word that describes the dales watered by these crystal streams.

In Narrowdale and Milldale, on the Dove, and in the gorge of the Wye above Monsal Dale, the banks of the streams approach the stern and gray order of river scenery. Here the waters have forced a channel betwixt limestone cliffs, with beetling crags and sheer escarpments. Amid surroundings more pastoral, the rivers flow on to the Trent, but in these lower lands there are spots of exceeding charm, and no lack of interest in the banks whereon the coarse-fisherman stands to watch his swan-quill, or to swing the bait for pike.

And like the country and the rivers, the trout and grayling fishing has a quaint fascination all its own. For Derbyshire angling is not quite the same affair as fly-fishing in the Test and Avon, nor is it exactly comparable with fishing in Yorkshire and the Northern Border streams. It is my conviction that the trout in question are better worth the angler's perseverance in attempting to lure them than the hungry, uneducated $\frac{1}{4}$-pounders of less-fished streams in Scotland and elsewhere.

If your object in fly-fishing is to make heavy baskets, with the minimum of skill, there are brooks in other parts of the United Kingdom where you may cast your three wet flies almost at random, and expect to hook a wee troutlet at about every other cast. This is one kind of trout-fishing, and I personally do not despise it upon occasion. But the well-earned, wary fish of

¾ pound in weight, which I have marked rising in the Dove, and hooked at the third or fourth transit of my olive dun on the outer ring of his dimple, gives me a keener satisfaction in the out-witting, and a livelier joy in the capture, than a dozen little trout from a burn.

This is not saying that fishing with the wet fly is impracticable in the rivers of Derbyshire. In the spring months, and at any time when the rivers are coloured, very good sport may be obtained by sinking the fly. Many of the local anglers never use the wet fly. They have been reared in the tradition of dry-fly fishing, and they profess ignorance of the methods of the sunk fly, while some of the craft hold such fishing in con-tempt.

Is this a reasonable prejudice ? The two oldest fly-fishermen in the county, Sir Thomas Wardle and John Fosbrooke of Hartington, water-keeper to the Trent Conservancy, both fish with the wet fly. Sir Thomas Wardle owns a length of the Dove above Dovedale, where the water is usually pellucid, and yet he makes heavy baskets with the wet fly. Fosbrooke ' never tinkers his fly,' to use his own phrase, but adheres valiantly to the older mode of fly-fishing. Both of these anglers could undoubtedly hold their own against dry-fly fishermen on their local streams. Therefore, if anyone informs you that no one can take trout with the wet fly in the Derbyshire rivers, do not heed him, but adapt your fishing to the water, the season of the year, and the general conditions.

In the Manifold I have had better sport with the wet fly than with the floating fly. I do not believe in that bigoted orthodoxy which announces that only the dry fly shall be used all the season round. What of chilly days in April, when one may look in vain for the rings of rising trout, and fail to discern any standing fish ?

Will you go home with an empty creel merely because you deem it heretical to throw a brace of small hackle flies off the edges of the streams ? If so, I am afraid that in certain seasons you will have very little fishing until the end of May, while in times of spate you will be forced to leave your rod at home in its canvas case. By changing my style of fishing from wet fly to dry fly, I can usually contrive to catch trout from the beginning of April until the end of September, and grayling from mid-June till Christmas.

I willingly agree that there is something extremely alluring and unique in dry-fly fishing. It is the finest poetry of fly-fishing. But I do not neglect the finest prose because I am fond of poetry. There is, to my mind, a curious warp in the angler who rigidly refuses to use the wet fly when the floating fly fails to attract fish. If it is a question of skill, I will go so far as to say, that in the limpid Wye it is easier to catch trout and grayling with the dry fly than with the sunk fly. Unless the water is thickly stained, wet-fly fishing is by no means a despicable art in these streams of the limestone region.

What, then, should be the fisherman's guide as to the mode of fly-fishing in Derbyshire ? My answer is that you should try either method, wet or dry, on the same day if need be. This is my own plan under certain conditions. For example, in the open length of the Wye, between Bakewell and Rowsley, I caught four brace of fish one day in the spring of 1904. Five out of the eight fish were taken with the wet fly. Some of these were hooked at the tail of runs, and the others in pools rippled by a breeze. You can soon discover whether trout are feeding near the surface.

If the duns are frisking prettily down a glide, and the trout are sucking them in, by all means oil your fly, stalk up, and let your lure float on the surface. The wet fly will hardly avail here unless the water is coloured. But if few flies or none can be seen, what do you propose to do ? You may peer about for standing fish, and try to tempt them with a floating fly, or you may pack up and go home. I do not propose to give up simply because I cannot use the dry fly. It is an easy operation to change the cast, and to fish with a couple of small flies in the sunk fashion. The trout may be feeding greedily on the larvæ under water. I would rather catch them on the surface, but I am not going to lose a half-day's sport because the trout will not rise to my floating blue dun or olive. As a keeper on the Dove remarked to me : ' This is the sort of day when you can *make* 'em rise to the wet fly.'

We will suppose, however, that you find your-self on the bank of the stream on a warm day at the close of June. The water is bright and rather low, and the sunshine is somewhat glaring. Here and there, on the stills by the boughs, good trout and grayling are rising to surface insects.

This is not a wet-fly day. You may get a brace
or two with wet fly late in the evening by fishing
in the runs, but the dry fly will be the only
effective method of tempting fish in the full
daylight. Therefore, mark your trout, and cast
the floating fly over them. If you have graduated
upon wet-fly rivers in the North, do not be dis-
couraged at the prospect. With a steady perseverance you will soon acquire the knack of
dropping your dry fly prettily, and in the right
spot.

I have watched a Scot, used to rough rivers
and wet-fly fishing, learn the trick of dry-fly
casting in one day by the Wye. Every wet-fly
angler has the root of the matter in him, and it
is only a question of practice to change from one
style to the other.

I have endeavoured to make clear that the
wet-fly fisherman need not be dismayed when
he is told that 'there is only dry-fly fishing in
Derbyshire.' There is almost any kind of fishing
which you may please to select. You may even
use the worm and minnow in certain parts, and
fish with float tackle for big trout at Matlock.
If you are already a dry-fly angler, well and good ;
you will need no tuition. If you cannot throw

a dry fly, you have a better chance of learning here than in the chalk streams of the South, and at much less cost. And should you ever have the fortune to fish the famous Hampshire rivers, you will assuredly derive profitable experience from dry-fly fishing in Derbyshire.

As compared with the rivers of Wales and the West of England, the streams of Derbyshire and Staffordshire must be described as 'late.' Although the Trent Conservators have fixed February 1 as the opening day for trout-fishing in the tributary streams, there is not much chance of successful fly-fishing until the second or third week in April. From that time onwards until the end of June the trout-fishing is usually at its best, though it happens in some years that spring frosts and east winds combine to mar sport in April. One cannot, however, prognosticate with any certainty as to good fishing days.

My best basket from the Dove last year was made on a day of bitterly cold wind in April, when snow seemed in the air, and I could scarcely keep warm in my winter clothes and a mackintosh. I have seen a good rise to fly early in March in the Lathkill, but that was upon one of those days of exceptional mildness that often precede a spell of cold, cheerless weather in the early spring.

July is a poor fishing month almost everywhere. Conditions often improve in August, and September may be even better. October is considered the best month for grayling-fishing, and in mid winter grayling can still be induced to rise to the fly between the hours of 12 p.m. and 3. With the sport of grayling and coarse-fishing in the drear months, and trout-fishing in the spring and summer, there is full scope for the fisherman in this locality to pursue his pastime throughout the year.

The Mayfly appears upon most of the lengths early in June, in favourable seasons. It is often plentiful on the Derwent, Wye, and Dove. Some years ago the erratic drake was not seen over the Manifold. Now, thanks to John Fosbrooke, who 'planted' a number of the pupæ in that stream, there is an annual hatch of the imago in the length near Hartington. In 'The Trout,' the Marquess of Granby refers to the disappearance of the Mayfly upon the Lathkill for some seasons past, though, oddly enough, the fly is very abundant over the tributary Bradford stream. So far as my observations go during 1904, the drakes hatched out

in fair numbers on the lower lengths of the Bradford, but very few were seen upon the dams near
Middleton. On the Upper Dove last season there
was a good show of Mayflies for about ten days,
and on two or three occasions trout rose to them
with huge avidity.

A few words upon tackle and flies may be of
use to the stranger in this district. An all-round
fly-rod, let it be of split cane or green-heart, should
be brought to Derbyshire. By an all-round rod
I mean one that will cast a dry fly as well as a
wet fly. A lissom weapon of 11 or 12 feet,
which may be admirably adapted for wet-fly
fishing, is not the rod for these rivers. What is
needed is a fairly stiff, but not stubborn, rod of
10 feet or even 9 feet in length. This will serve
for either style of fly-fishing. The line may be
fairly heavy, and if tapered so much the better.
Casts must be fine for clear-water fishing. They
may also be tapered. And it is well to have one
or two casts of the finest drawn gut in readiness.

Reels may be of any make favoured by the pre-
dilection of the fisherman, and the same may be
said for landing-nets. Wading-stockings, and for
preference wading-trousers, are necessary ad-
juncts to fly-fishing in the Derwent from What-

standwell to the higher lengths. Wading is not allowed in the Duke of Rutland's length of the Wye, nor is it essential to wade in parts of the Dove nor in the Manifold. Anglers who kneel to make their casts should protect the knees with pads or wading-stockings. These protections may prevent a case of rheumatism.

The subject of flies provides a theme of universal interest to trout and grayling fishermen. Derbyshire, like other parts of the kingdom, has its ' local patterns ' of artificial flies. For wet-fly fishing hackle flies are to be preferred, and they should be dressed on rather small hooks. I have used the Yorkshire hackles with success in the Wye, Derwent, Dove, and Manifold. For the last river, Fosbrooke ties some quaint and killing patterns, much resembling the insect as it emerges from the pupa. One of his lures, which may be used wet for trout and grayling, he has dubbed the Golden Earwig. It is a good general fly for the Manifold and Upper Dove. Messrs. Foster and Co., of Ashbourne, have a number of specialities for the Derbyshire streams, which they guarantee to kill fish. Eaton, of Matlock, can be relied upon to dress flies for the Derwent and Wye. He is a good fisherman of

long experience.   Allen, who watches the Darley
Club length of the Derwent, is another fly-tier
who can be recommended.   He lives at Rowsley.
Lock, the keeper, Load Mill, Alstonefield, ties
excellent flies for the Dove.   Wood and Co., of
Pinstone Street, Sheffield, who turn out good fly-
rods at reasonable prices, can advise as to the
best patterns of flies for the higher Derwent and
its tributaries, and the streams over the Yorkshire border.*   Such flies as the yellow dun, olive
dun, ash dun, apple green, gravel bed, iron-blue
dun, furnace bumble, and claret bumble are tied
locally, and have points of their own differentiat-
ing them from the patterns known commercially
by these names.   The best flies are not always
the most lovely to look upon, and the cheapest
flies are usually the dearest in the long-run.   I
do not wish to restrict the experimental fisherman to the use of the flies that I have enumerated.
Let him try anything and everything.   But I
think he will waste his time if he tries to tempt
the Derbyshire trout with big palmers, zulus,
coch-y-bonddus, stone-flies, and daddy-long-legs.

Upon the whole, the visitor may be guided by

* See complete list of local fly-tiers at the end of the
book.

2

the experience of local anglers. Pale and dark
olive duns, used dry, account for many good fish
in Derbyshire. A little later on the yellow dun
may be used in two sizes. The larger fly serves
well about dusk, or upon very windy days, and
in heavy water. A capital emergency fly is the
iron blue. On dull days by the Wye I have seen
the naturals come out in processions between
fitful batches of olive duns. At such times
nothing but the iron blue will tickle the palate
of the fastidious trout. Olives are then scornfully refused. It is, therefore, advisable to carry
a supply of the useful iron blue at all times.

As to Mayflies, do not use them very big or
very gaudy in the dressing. They should float
and cock well, and resemble the natural fly as
closely as possible. The spent gnat should not
be forgotten. Do not be surprised, however, if
your cunningest Mayfly is rejected, even in the
midst of a big flight of the real insect. Trout are
apt to exhibit singular caprice in the Mayfly
season. But as a rule fish are on the look-out
at this carnival time, and you may confidently
use any other fly which is in season if the drake
is refused.

I think I have generalized quite enough concerning the flies for this district. The rest may well be left to the fisherman's judgment. I will now reply to the possible query as to whether the rivers are over-fished. My answer is that this may be true of one or two lengths close to towns, but, upon the whole, fishermen certainly do not jostle one another upon the banks. Naturally, the trout of much-fished waters are more intelligent than those of lonely lochs and unfrequented mountain burns. Personally, I would describe the fly-fishing in Derbyshire as extremely fascinating by reason of the conditions which I have endeavoured to make plain in the preceding pages. It is the kind of fly-fishing that has attracted a very large number of men whose names are well known at the Fly-fishers' Club and among anglers generally. I need only mention the Marquess of Granby (whose preserves on the Lathkill and Bradford afford splendid fishing), Lord John Manners, Sir Thomas Wardle, Mr. William Senior (Editor of the *Field*), Mr. John Bickerdyke, Mr. Rolt, Mr. R. B. Marston, Mr. Paul Taylor, and Mr. Longman.

The system of fish preservation in Derbyshire is generally good. There are trout hatcheries on the Dove, two on the Lathkill, and one on the

Matlock Association length of the Derwent. A number of private ponds have been stocked with rainbow and Loch Leven trout, but the latter species has not thrived when introduced to the Lathkill. Two or more water-keepers are employed constantly on the several club waters of the Derwent. The Wye is well watched from below Buxton to its junction with the Derwent at Rowsley, and all the private lengths are carefully protected. The upper Dove and the Manifold are free from coarse fish, except a few eels, and scaly enemies of trout are not abundant in the Derwent above Cromford. A few pike find their way into the Derwent from the Cromford Canal, but they are wired or netted at sight, and every means is taken to prevent their increase in trout waters. In the Wye, below Haddon, I have seen a few perch ; but in this well-stocked river they work but little damage, and are said to return periodically to the pond where they are bred. Chub are scarce in the Derwent above Matlock, and are not often seen in the Wye. Here, as elsewhere, herons and aquatic birds account for the destruction of a certain number of fish and of the ova. Dabchicks are rather too abundant on the upper Bradford.

Pollutions from mills and manufactories work some measure of mischief along parts of the mid and lower Derwent, and drainage and contamination below Buxton have affected a portion of the Wye. The Dove and Manifold are free from pollution in their trout and grayling yielding reaches. A long length of the Churnet has been ruined by mill pollution.

Poaching fish is a rather uncommon offence in Derbyshire rivers. There is but little tampering with trout on the spawning redds, as the rivers are too well guarded. The nefarious fishing is almost entirely confined to the laying down of night-lines, and this is not a very common practice. Some years ago the upper Dove was poached with nets a few miles below its source, and I have heard stories of trout-spearing by night in this quarter. But as compared with Wales, fish-poaching in Derbyshire is almost harmless.

In the last report of the Trent Conservators reference is made to sewage pollution at Bakewell. It is difficult to say whether the crude sewage works real harm among the trout and grayling of the Wye. The water has been carefully analyzed at the mouth of the sewer, and also a hundred yards below the effluent, and the analyst pronounces it free from elements noxious to fish. A brook at Cromford is described as ' very bad,' and an order has been made for a sewage scheme at Matlock.

The Earl of Harrington has recently received damages from the Corporation of Derby for pollution of certain fish-ponds upon his estate. At Belper new sewage works are in the course of construction. The report states : ' The district has been especially free from serious pollutions and offences. Some old-standing pollutions are being dealt with, and upon others pressure is being brought to bear.'

The heaviest penalty imposed for illicit fishing during the year 1903 was £5 and £1 5s. costs. This was a case of night-lining heard at Ashbourne

The owners of private fisheries on the Dove, Manifold, Wye, Lathkill, and Bradford constantly restock their waters. Some lengths of these rivers literally swarm with well-fed, takeable trout from about 7 ounces up to a couple of pounds in weight. There are, of course, bigger trout in all these rivers. Perhaps 8 to 10 ounces is a fair average to fix upon for the trout of the district. In the Manifold the average weight is probably less, but trout and grayling are there very abundant and free-rising. A little length of the Bradford, which I am privileged to fish through the kindness of a neighbour, holds trout of an average weight of over ¾ pound.

It is curious, upon looking through my fishing diary, to find how many of the trout from this length weigh just under 1 pound. My biggest fish caught this year (1904) scaled 2¼ pounds, and a few trout of 2 pounds were taken last year from this part of the Bradford. In this stream one rarely catches a trout weighing less than 9 ounces.

In my account of the various rivers, I will refer to the captures of big trout and grayling. There are some veritable monsters in the Wye, and each year the Matlock waters yield about a score of fine trout well over 2 pounds in weight.

The close times for fish in the Trent Fishery District are as follows :

Salmon, with nets, between September 1 and February 1, both inclusive.
Salmon, with rod, between November 2 and February 1, both inclusive.
Trout and char, between October 2 and February 1, both inclusive.
Grayling and coarse fish, between March 15 and June 15, both inclusive.

Licenses must be produced when demanded by a conservator, water-bailiff, constable, or licensee, under a penalty of £1, and the holder can require anyone he finds fishing to produce his license, which cannot be transferred. All unseasonable fish and young fry taken accidentally must be returned to the water with the least possible injury, or the taker will be liable to a penalty. The clerk to the Trent Fishery Board is Mr. C. K. Eddowes, 2, The Strand, Derby.

CHAPTER II

SWEET is the name of this stream in the ear of the angler. The Dove! Who among the fraternity of piscators has not longed to roam in Walton's footsteps, and to cast his fly upon the gently-swirling flood between the gray crags of Dovedale? Sooner or later every fly-fisher feels impelled to make a pilgrimage to the Dove.

> ' Oh, my beloved Nymph! fair Dove!
> Princess of rivers! How I love
>   Upon thy flowing banks to lie,
> And view thy silver stream !
> When gilded by a summer's beam !
>   And in it all thy wanton fry
> Playing at liberty ;
> And, with my angle upon them,
>   The all of treachery
>   I ever learned industriously to try.'

So sang Charles Cotton in his ' irregular stanzas ' addressed to Mr. Izaak Walton. Other pens, in poetry and prose, have written in praise of Cotton's 'beloved Dove,' and many deft painters have depicted the beauties of Derbyshire's most famous dale.

Is it from the burden and coo of its flow that the Dove derives its name ? It is more probable that Dove is a modernized form of the old Celtic *dur*, meaning water. We find the root in *Der*went and *Dart*, and, according to Dr. Isaac Taylor, in Dover or *Dur*beck in Nottinghamshire. Then why not in Dove ? From its source, on the slope of Axe Edge, down to the confluence with the Trent, the Dove is a charming and a fishful stream. In its stripling career the river meanders from the uplands to water a green vale below the shapely hills of Chrome, Hollins, and Parkhouse, and on by High Wheeldon to the bridge at Crowdecote. Thus far the Dove yields only small trout here and there in times of rainy weather. From its first mill onwards the volume of water increases, and there are, no doubt, a few good trout in some of the dubs. There is, however, little fishing until the stream emerges into the secluded valley below Crowdecote. Here, for about three miles of its course, on the right bank, the Dove is owned by Mr. Charles Finney, of Broadmeadow Hall, the representative of an old yeoman family who have occupied the ancient manor-house for many years. The fishing and shooting rights were in the market in the spring of 1904, and were let to a Leicester gentleman.

Opposite Broadmeadow is one of the Duke of Devonshire's farms, called Pilsbury, and now in the hands of Mr. Bunting. The farm doubtless derives its name from Pilsbury Castle, an ancient fortification, with a mound, ditch, and vallum, which overlooks the winding stream, and commands an enchanting view of the cluster of sharp hills near Longnor. The Pilsbury right extends on the left bank for about a mile and a half. I was part lessee of this length during 1904, which proved to be one of the dryest summers known in Derbyshire for many years past. At the time of writing I cannot say who will rent this water during 1905, but the lessor reserves to himself the right of granting fishing leave to anyone staying at Pilsbury, where there is comfortable accommodation in a large homestead. The nearest railway - station is Hurdlow, on the Buxton and Ashbourne line, but for driving Hartington is the better point of arrival.

The Dove in this quiet vale of Pilsbury is a

narrow winding stream, with some pools of from
3 to 5 feet in depth, occasional scours, and a
number of shallow broken runs. It is rather
thickly overgrown on the banks, which have,
for some distance, the disadvantage of being a
few feet above the level of the brook. This
necessitates crouching and stalking up to rising
fish, or very cautious wading up-stream. Some
good fish, especially grayling, haunt the deep
pools. I saw a remarkable rise on this length
during the Mayfly season, when fish appeared
to be in every part of the stream. When the
water is low and bright only a few trout and
small grayling venture to show themselves on the
shallows. I discovered that the fish in this stream
make habitual use of the numerous water-vole
holts under the water. Very often a hooked
trout bores away for one of these holes, and
gets his snout into it before you can check him.
There is plenty of harbourage, and no lack of
bottom food for both trout and grayling in this
part of the Dove. John Fosbrooke tells me that
these are about the best-fed fish in the Dove.

The exceptionally low state of the stream
prevented me from forming a very precise
opinion upon the sport that one should expect in

a normal season. I took some fair grayling with the fly up to 1 pound in weight, and rather fewer trout. The trout average 6 ounces, and occasionally one gets a fish of ¾ pound. They rise pretty freely to the wet fly in April during dull, windy weather, but as the season wears on the dry fly is more effective. The best flies are the iron-blue dun, blue dun, olive dun, yellow dun, and small black gnat. Fosbrooke's golden earwig will kill here after a spate. Any of the ordinary grayling flies will serve in October. There is a good run for grayling at the bend at the top of Bunting's length, near a partly-submerged fallen tree, and also in the tails of the pools below it. Near the old camp there is a pool, with a sunken rock in it, which is generally good for a trout or two. Lower down is a deep hole, which I christened the Rock Pool. It is difficult to fish from the bank, but easy to cast into from the shallow tail end. This pool, which has a high bank on the Pilsbury side, is full of grayling, and it is seldom that one fails to see the rings of rises. A wide run below, near a cattle drinking-place, is a favourable spot for trout. There is a strip of island at the end of the run. Some good grayling and trout frequent the runs above the ford and the wooden foot-bridge. We have now reached the end of the Broadmeadow and Pilsbury lengths. A fair number of the turned-in trout, including a few rainbows, work their way up to this water from Hartington and Beresford Dale. There are some good spawning-grounds in this part of the river. To sum up, I may say that baskets of eight or a dozen trout of a take-able size may occasionally be made in this length with the fly. I have not used the worm here for trout, but preceding tenants have done so, and no doubt accounted for good catches. The best catch which I inspected last season was taken with the Mayfly, partly in this length and the length just below. It numbered fifteen trout, some of them weighing over $\frac{1}{2}$ pound. The biggest grayling recorded last year scaled $1\frac{1}{2}$ pounds, and it was taken with the fly. I have little doubt that there are some trout of 2 pounds in some of the deeper dubs hereabouts. I am told that a trout weighing 3 pounds was caught half a mile below during 1904.

Very much depends upon the volume of water in this part of the Dove, and unless there is a good stream running, the day's take to the fly will probably not be more than two brace. At any rate, these will not be the insignificant trout or grayling of a mountain burn.

After the ford below Pilsbury and Broad-meadow, the Dove roams in a serpentine course down to Ludwell Mill and Hartington Village. There are perhaps more fish in this length, as the river is wider and deeper, and parts below have been heavily stocked. The fishing here is let by the farmers by the season, and short reaches can sometimes be secured early in the spring. Intending lessees may communicate with me.

At Hartington, a charming village, with a hotel, an inn, a post-office, and some boarding-houses, the fisherman will find very pleasant head-quarters. The village is about a mile from the station, and the hotel omnibus meets all trains. For the upper Dove and parts of the Manifold Hartington is a good centre. Fishermen should write to John Fosbrooke, who lives in this village, and inquire as to the state of the rivers. This veteran is in a position enabling him to give valuable advice, as he has fished these waters for very many years, and acted as water-bailiff to Sir Vauncey Crewe and the Conservators of the Trent District.

The Charles Cotton Hotel at Hartington is a

well-known house for visitors and anglers. It is three-quarters of a mile from Beresford Dale, and close to the Dove. The proprietor has the right of fishing upon a short length, containing trout and grayling. No charge is made for the fishing to visitors at the hotel. Day tickets for non-residents at the house cost half a crown. Dry or wet fly can be used.*

From Hartington down to the romantic defile of Beresford Dale the Dove meanders through pleasant meadows. We now reach a long portion of strictly preserved private water, abounding with trout and grayling. The riparian owner of the right bank is Sir Vauncey Crewe, and the left bank belongs to the Challoner family, who let the water to Mr. Frank Green. This gentleman has repeatedly stocked the water with rainbow and other kinds of trout.

At Beresford Dale we come in sight of Charles Cotton's famous fishing-house, which stands on an island at the head of the charming little ravine. The public footpath is on the left bank, but we soon cross the bridge at the Pike Pool, and follow

* Accommodation can also be obtained at the Hartington Hall boarding - house (with fishing), and at Mr. Low's comfortable farm-house close to the village.

the right bank for awhile. This little dale is reminiscent of Walton and Cotton, and every fisherman should visit the spot, even though he may not fish the stream.

Crossing again to the left bank at the end of Beresford Dale, we reach the fine gorge of Narrow Dale, a gray scene on a dull day, but at no time devoid of beauty. The river has been artificially dammed here, and it would be hard to find a prettier length for fly-fishing. We shall see plenty of fish rising in the tails of the pools, and may catch sight of some very plump grayling and goodly trout. Sir Thomas Wardle owns the fishing here on the right bank, and below, on the opposite side, the water is rented by Mr. Hall.

These enthusiastic anglers have done much to improve the fishing in this length. Sir Thomas Wardle has a stock pool, in which he successfully breeds rainbow, Loch Leven, fontinalis, and native brown trout. The average weight of the trout in this length is from 9 to 10 ounces, and the grayling average rather more in weight.

About two miles down we come to wooded slopes, and banks of a more diversified character. Sir Thomas Wardle's luncheon-hut is on the right bank, and his preserve is continued down

3

t below Load Mill.   We have now entered Milldale, at the head of Dovedale.

A length of about one mile on the left bank can
be fished by visitors at the New Inn Hotel, Alsop-
en-le-Dale,* a comfortable house on the Buxton
and Ashbourne Road, and about one and a quarter
miles from the river.

There is a good stock of trout and grayling in
this pretty stretch, and the banks are fairly open.
Day tickets are issued at 1s. 6d.

Mounting a cliff path above a deep pool, we
soon come in view of Ilam Rock and the upper
part of Dovedale.   The queen of the Derbyshire
dales deserves a chapter to herself.

* The   proprietor   is   Mr.   Colin   Prince.   Station
(L. & N.W.R.) close to the house.

CHAPTER III

FISHING IN DOVEDALE

DOVEDALE proper, the holiday elysium of anglers, tourists, and amateur photographers, is that fine ravine stretching betwixt rock, wood, scree, and steeply-sloping sward from Ilam Rock to the two sentinel hills of Thorpe Cloud and Bunster. The dale is about two miles long, and within that distance is concentrated all that makes the varied beauty of a Highland glen, a Welsh mountain gorge, and a Devonshire cleave.

'Bless me! what mountains are here! Are we not in Wales?' cried the delighted Viator in Charles Cotton's portion of 'The Complete Angler.'

'No,' answered Piscator, 'but in almost as mountainous a country.'

Undoubtedly, the view looking up the gully, from the knoll upon which stands the Izaak Walton Hotel, is fairly comparable with many

gorge scenes in North Wales.   But Dovedale has
a character all its own.   The river is charmingly
adapted by Nature and aided by art for the sport
of fly-fishing.   In this two-mile length of renowned water there is but little rough scrambling
for the wielder of the rod.   The banks are dry,
and of firm turf, pleasant to tread upon, while
only a few bushes in the lower length impede
casting.   A weir here and there breaks the course
of the merry, sparkling stream, and an occasional
boulder makes a twin current beloved of trout.
For such as like to wade among rocks and to cast
in the shadow of trees there is scope at the upper
end of the dale.   The more sedate angler, the
votary of the dry fly, who stalks his trout and
grayling, will find stretches to his fancy in the
middle and lower lengths of the dale water.
Nature has made this stream for the fisherman.
It is perhaps the most tempting river in all
England.

Dovedale is owned by two or three families.
The Hanburys of Ilam Hall possess a share on
the Staffordshire side, and the Fitzherbert family
claim a part of the Derbyshire (left) bank.   The
fishing is granted on the right bank to the Izaak
Walton Hotel, which we shall presently visit, and

on a length of the left bank to the Peveril of the Peak Hotel. The latter hostelry is a little distance from the river, on the way to Thorpe Cloud Station. It is a big house, providing entertainment for a large number of guests from Easter till the autumn. Day tickets for the left bank from the Stepping Stones up to Dove Holes are issued at the Peveril and the Dog and Partridge, near Thorpe Station, at 1s. 6d. a day.

On the right, or Staffordshire, side the whole of the fishing from Ilam Rock to the junction of the Dove and Manifold is in the privilege of Mr. W. Evans, proprietor of the Izaak Walton Hotel. The river, upon entering Dovedale, flows between high cliffs, and is of a rushing and broken character. To fish here wading is necessary, but the stream soon emerges and widens out to pretty runs and pools, where casting is comfortable, not to say luxurious. A broad 'flat,' containing some fine trout and grayling, succeeds the series of weirs, until we reach the Stepping Stones. This slowly-moving pool provides good fly-fishing when agitated by a breeze. Near the Stepping Stones, where the stream takes a sudden bend to the right, there is a formidable barrier, known as the Iron Gate. The gate is closed to the day-tripper, as there is no public footpath on this bank of the stream, but the key is kept at the Izaak Walton Hotel.

We have now reached the lower stretch of this water. The Dove flows swiftly, in a straighter course, through a deep gully with bare, rocky slopes, much frequented by rabbits. Every yard of this reach is fishable with the fly, and fish lurk by almost every stone in the river's bed. When the water is low, in times of long drought, scores, if not hundreds, of trout and grayling may be counted. Passing under a wooden foot-bridge, the Dove takes leave of the rugged dale, and winds through meadows down to the junction of the Manifold. This part is less open, but with wading-stockings one can command almost all the fishable corners.

The left bank of the river in the gully belongs to the Okeover Fishing Club, who also own the fishing on the opposite bank of the Manifold from Ilam Bridge down to below Mappleton on the Dove. This water has been stocked with rainbow trout. The preserve is only open to members, and at the present time I believe that the club is restricted to seven anglers.

The fishing from the left bank of the Manifold,

from Ilam Bridge to the confluence with the Dove, belongs to the Izaak Walton Hotel. There is another stretch of the hotel water on the Dove, a short distance below the mouth of the Manifold, and on the left bank. This is known as the Broadlow Ash length. It is well stocked with fish, but the overgrown banks necessitate wading. With these lengths on the Dove and Manifold the water in the hotel right affords about five miles of fishing.

And now a few words as to the quality of the fishing. Frankly, this is not the place for the man who fishes only for the basket, nor for the raw beginner possessed of scanty patience. No one expects to fill a creel with the singularly wary fish of this much-fished and pellucid water. It is a sportsman's length, the scene of careful stalking and cunning casting on the part of those highly-proficient habitués who make their home at the Izaak Walton for a month or longer at a stretch.

I do not mean to lay it down as an axiom that a fair hand with a couple of flies, fished wet in the more broken streams, will be utterly outclassed by the mediocre artist with the dry fly. In early spring, and in the winter - grayling season, fish can be taken here with the wet fly.

It is, however, a matter of creed with certain of the regular visitors at the 'Walton' never to stoop, even at the worst of times, to the usage of a sunk fly. If the trout or grayling distinctly refuse to rise, these stern devotees prefer not to catch fish. They apply themselves to golf, or to gossip in the garden, and speculate upon the chance of an evening rise.

Dovedale is an excellent school for the fly-fisherman. Every member of the gentle craft should go thither at least once or twice in the course of his life. He will learn what education does for trout, and even for the less diffident grayling, and he will see some of the cleverest anglers to be found in the British Islands, men who can outwit the knowingest old wiseacre of a fish. Here you may win *kudos*, and gain your claim to recognition as a real fisherman.

Sooner or later, if you make a study of this advanced fishing, you will meet with success. Then great will be your triumph, far excelling that of the wet-fly man, who carries home 6 or 8 pounds of trout from a peat-stained, broken river. For you have entered into competition with trout that know the look of an artificial fly as well as you do, and you have taken, by the employment of the finest of piscatorial art, a couple of brace of handsome, distinguished, cultured fish. You may flatter yourself that you are now no fool at this engrossing game. You have pitted your skill with trout worthy of your art and perseverance. At night, in the cosy, old-fashioned smoking-room, you will be received into the innermost circle of the adepts.

If once an angler falls in love with the fair nymph Dove, he will court her favours with a supreme ardour. His heart will stir at the sound of her name, and he will long to heed again the tender burden of her song. She is a sweet mistress, though she has her moods and wayward spells. You must woo her with ardent persistence.

Are you weary of the 'desk's dull drudgery' and the fierce scramble for subsistence in the dingy town? Then hie to Dovedale, and dream, and fish, and seek right good company at the Izaak Walton. The moorland air will recuperate you, and send sound slumber by night, and the stalking and casting from ten in the morning till six in the evening will give you tone in less than a week. Are you past the years when a man can climb rocks, and stand all day up to his waist in a strong rush of cold water? Then take your pleasure with the angle upon a stream with open, level banks, and mark your trout as they rise on the shady opposite side of the gently-swirling pools of the Dove.

With what flies shall we seek to tempt these lusty fish of Dovedale ? Wait until you are upon the scene, and ascertain then what the adepts are using. Yet I would impress upon you that no hard-and-fast laws need cumber your mind. The host will sell you the flies that have proved 'killers.' For the rest, employ your own discretion, remembering what I have written on this subject in the opening chapter.

The trout in this water average rather over ½ pound. Fish of 1 pound are fairly common. The grayling, which appear to be more abundant than the trout, average 9 or 10 ounces. Trout have been caught up to 1 pound 10 ounces, grayling up to 1¾ pounds. Pound grayling are numerous. Some time ago the gully-length yielded fourteen brace of fish to one rod in a day. Eight brace is reckoned a capital catch for a day's angling. During the last Mayfly season four rods made an average total catch of fifty-four brace in about ten days.

Bait and minnow fishing are forbidden in this

preserve, and no fish measuring less than 10 inches may be retained.

The comfortable Izaak Walton is in an amphitheatre of picturesque hills. It stands on a knoll, washed at the foot by the Dove and Manifold. Thorpe Station is about two miles away. The postal address is 'Ilam, near Ashbourne,' and the telegraph-office is at Fenny Bentley. Tickets for trout and grayling fishing are 1s. per day for the Dove only, and 2s. for the whole length of water. By the week the charge is 3s. 6d. for part of the preserve, and 7s. 6d. for the Dove and Manifold. Fishing permits are only issued to visitors at the hotel.

'Well, go thy way, little Dove!' quoth Viator; 'thou art the finest river that ever I saw, and the fullest of fish.'

The trout-fishing in Dovedale and on the Manifold is generally at its best from April till the end of June. Grayling begin to rise well in August and September, and better still in October. In November they are in the pink of condition, and will take either a dry or wet fly between mid-day and three o'clock. A fair hatch of duns and other flies may often be seen upon the Dove, on mild days, up to Christmas.

CHAPTER IV

THE DOVE : ROCESTER TO UTTOXETER

WE have traced the Dove from its source to below Dovedale and the confluence of the Manifold. Between this point and Rocester, on the North Staffordshire Railway, a portion of the stream is rented by the limited Okeover Club, while other lengths are in private hands. Rocester is a small village close to the junction of the Churnet with the Dove.* It is twenty minutes' walk to Dove Bridge at Rocester, where, on the east side, three fields below the bridge, is the boundary of the Uttoxeter Angling Association water. The Dove length extends to one field above Dove Bridge, Uttoxeter, on the east side, on the Eaton Estate.

This club has the fishing right over more than eight miles of the Dove, Churnet, and Tean Brook. The entrance-fee to the association is £1, and the

* Accommodation at Railway Hotel, near station.

annual subscription £2 2s. Sergeant-Major Garwood, Uttoxeter, is the honorary secretary. The
length limit for trout and grayling is 7 inches,
and there is no restriction upon the size of coarse
fish. Trout-fishing begins March 1, and the fly
and artificial minnow can be used on the brooks
after June 30. All-round fishing is permitted in
the Dove. Day permits, obtainable from Messrs.
Foster, Ashbourne, or the Secretary, Uttoxeter,
cost 2s. 6d. per day. These tickets are not
available for the Tean Brook during June.

This is a pleasant length to fish, as the banks
are open almost throughout the preserve. It
contains more grayling than trout, the former
being abundant. Maggot-fishing in the autumn
accounts for some fair baskets of grayling from
this water, and there is often a good rise to fly.
The Tean Brook, which affords sport when there
is a good supply of water, joins the Dove about
midway between Rocester and Uttoxeter. It
rises above Cheadle, in Staffordshire.

The character of the water is varied ; there
are sharp bends with scours, and rather long pools
of deep water. Below the inflow of the Churnet
the river is wider, and has at most times a good
current of water. Uttoxeter is perhaps the most

convenient centre for fishing this length.*   This
is a quiet market-town, with pastoral surroundings.

The Churnet has fallen upon evil days.   From
Leek downwards throughout its course, which
lies amid some of the prettiest scenery in England,
the river is badly polluted by dye-works and
paper-mills.   There is a steady decrease of fish
in this stream, and for angling purposes it is
practically ruined.   Before this contamination of
a beautiful and sport-giving tributary, trout bred
abundantly in its waters, and fish up to 3½ pounds
in weight were caught with the fly in the neighbourhood of Cheddleton.   Local anglers deplore
this despoiling of a charming river, but up to the
present there does not seem to be any proposal
for removing the nuisance.

The wet fly is employed in the Uttoxeter
water, some fishermen using three flies on a long
cast.   This is a profitable method of fishing in
the late autumn, when grayling are on the feed,
and it is more successful, upon the whole, than
dry-fly angling.   There are, however, resident
fishermen who prefer the dry fly all the year round.

* Accommodation : White Hart Hotel ; Talbot Inn
(clean and old-fashioned).

The coarse fish in this part of the Dove are pike, perch, and chub. Roach and very fine dace are abundant in some portions of the association preserve. The Uttoxeter club have also the right over a length of the Churnet in its lower part, where it is unaffected by pollution. Sergeant-Major Garwood informs me that he takes good grayling and dace from this length.

The association water on the Tean Brook begins at Fole Mill, four miles from Uttoxeter, on the Cheadle Road, and extends to within two miles of Uttoxeter.

These waters are being restocked (1904) with many hundreds of two-year-old trout. This will no doubt restore the balance between the trout and grayling in the preserve. It will be seen from these notes on the lower Dove and its tributaries that there is varied sport for fishermen in the neighbourhood of Uttoxeter.

CHAPTER V

THE MANIFOLD

THIS stream, the sweet companion of the Dove, is the offspring of the bleak, high moors of Staffordshire, near to the isolated village of Flash. It rises from a hillside, nearly 1,500 feet above the level of the sea, and runs down through wild country to the green and more cultivated vale of Longnor. Born close to the source of the Dove, the Manifold may be said to bear that river company until it merges its waters with the ampler Dove below Ilam Hall. At Longnor the two streams are only one mile asunder, while they are even nearer at certain points in the lower reaches of the Manifold.

This delightful river receives more tributaries than the Dove in its higher lengths, while its water is rather more tinted, except in the dryest seasons. It is a less 'difficult' river than the

48

Dove, both by reason of its slight colour, and the fact that its trout are, upon the whole, less educated and cunning.

My own experience proves that the Manifold will yield, at any time of the trout and grayling seasons, about twice the number of fish that one may reasonably hope to catch from the Dove in a day's fishing. I think there is little doubt that the Manifold, from Longnor down to the confluence with the Dove at Ilam, breeds more trout and grayling than the latter river. In weight the fish of the Manifold will be found to average rather less than those of the Dove. Therefore, generally speaking, the Manifold will be preferred by those anglers who think that quantity compensates for quality.

In the upper Manifold the trout are perhaps the freest rising fish in the district under survey. I do not claim that they come quite so wildly to the artificial fly as the troutlets of certain Scottish or Welsh mountain brooks, but upon occasion the Manifold trout rise almost recklessly either to a sunk or floating fly. As for the grayling, they are bigger in the average than the trout, and when they are on the feed, you will find very few dull intervals during the day. Unfortunately the

4

grayling often take the fly eagerly during the close time, and frequently remain obdurate to the fisherman's wiles in the open season.

On April 27, 1904, I fished the Manifold for a few hours, when very few natural flies were visible on the surface of the stream. The water was rather low, the wind blew from the north-west, and the day was dull and chilly. My basket was nine grayling and six trout. The fly most favoured by the grayling was the blue dun. Almost all the grayling excelled the trout in weight, and had it not been the close season, I could have carried home a very pretty sample of Manifold grayling. Upon my next visit to this stream, on May 10, I took eleven fish—ten trout and only one grayling. Such is the variability of the elusive thymallus ! As the spring wears on the grayling do not rise quite so freely, but with the coming of August they begin to feed again upon surface-food.

The Manifold is an earlier river than the Dove. It sometimes gives sport with the fly in March, and as the grayling will rise all the year round, there is always fishing in the Manifold. John Fosbrooke, who has had many years on this stream and its tributaries, says that he has 'pulled out grayling hand over hand,' while standing nearly up to his knees in snow.

When casting on the Manifold I am always reminded of two Welsh streams which it resembles in the character of its water and its productiveness. These are the Ceirw and the Ceiriog. But the Manifold has this advantage over the Ceiriog: that throughout most of its course it is fairly free from impeding branches and undergrowth. The Manifold is, indeed, a very fishable stream from Longnor down to Hartington, the hindrances in casting being rarely insurmountable. For this reason it is a good school for the moderately experienced fly-fisherman, and even for the beginner.

Almost the whole of the Manifold is in the fishing right of Sir Vauncey Crewe, Bart. Sir Thomas Wardle rents a length below Hartington, and there are one or two short pieces of freehold land on its banks, whose owners claim the fishing. There is, however, an excellent stretch open to visitors who stay at the Crewe and Harpur Arms at Longnor. This outlying village, or small town, is seven miles from Buxton and about three from Hurdlow Station. I agree with Baddeley's 'Guide to the Peak District' that Longnor should be 'a much more favourite halting-place for tourists than it has hitherto been.' It is a quaint townlet, perched high on the ridge dividing the valleys of the Dove and the Manifold, and surrounded by wild and beautiful country. The air is bracing and cool in summer, and there are the charms of seclusion and serenity about the place.

The Manifold Valley Railway will open up this Arcadia, which has hitherto remained unexplored, save by a few pedestrian or cyclist tourists. It will be many years, let us hope, before the commercial speculator erects mills and factories in the sequestered vales of this thinly-peopled district. The ancient savour of days when Charles Cotton lived at Beresford Hall, and Izaak Walton wandered by the Dove, still clings to these dales and moorlands. One meets with natives whose dialect is archaic and unfamiliar to the ears of townsmen. Primitive customs prevail among these sturdy folk, whose bluff, independent demeanour must not be mistaken for rudeness. The women wear sunbonnets and clatter along on clogs. At the old farm-houses you will be well served from an ample larder. Hot cakes of various sorts appear at the tea-hour ; the home-cured ham is tender, and the cream fresh and delicious.

Except in the height of the holiday season there is no rush of fishermen to the open lengths of the Manifold. It is not a river for the day angler, who comes in the morning and goes by rail in the evening, but for the more leisurely fisherman who can spare a week or so. The more famous Dove allures a larger number of fishermen.

In the Wye and the ticket lengths of the Dove the trout have a trick of rising with extreme caution and scornfully refusing the fly. The Manifold trout rise with more boldness, but for all that they are not the easiest of prey. At any rate, on the poorest day you will not fail to excite a few fish into rising, and under propitious conditions you may expect a pretty basket. Seven grayling, including one of $1\frac{1}{2}$ pounds, in half an hour, from one little pool, is not a bad score, and it is not an unusual one on the Manifold.

I would choose to be by this merry little river at the latter end of April, on a dull warm day. Spring fly-fishing is charming here. A large variety of flies are hatched out from the Manifold. In one day I have noted ten different insects flying over the stream. April brings the blue dun, and a little later the olive dun appears. I have not seen March browns in any abundance. If the wind changes to a cold quarter during the day, by all means put on the iron-blue dun, dressed by Fosbrooke of Hartington. Bumbles and small hackles may be used wet in the early months. I have taken fish on the dry fly in April, but, as a rule, the trout do not rise steadily to the floating fly until the middle of May.

Those who despise the method of ranging and trying the tails of the runs with two or three wet flies should wait until a spell of warm weather has brought the fish well to the surface. Grayling are to be sought almost everywhere in summer, but the biggest are usually taken from the deeper pools fringed with alder-bushes. None of the quiet pools should be passed by on a breezy day. I have taken some good fish from the long stills on windy days by letting my flies sink and working them slowly under water.

In some lengths the banks are three or more feet above the level of the stream. Do not stand on the edge of the bank with the sun behind you, and wave an 11-feet rod across the streamlet. In that 4-inch deep run there are at least a dozen standing fish, and every one of them will see your silhouette against the sky, unless you climb down and stalk upstream to them. Here, as in the upper Dove, you will put down scores of fish if you are too lazy to get on a level with the river. You need not fall in, as I did one day last spring, after dancing for half a minute on a slimy stone.

They breed bulls hereabouts. It is just as well to keep a corner of your eye on the near pasture. I was once compelled to beat a strategic retreat across the river to avoid the pleasantries of an agile young bull, who warned me with a thundering bellow after quietly stalking up to within a couple of yards from me. No doubt it was 'only play,' but what is sport to bulls is sometimes death to men.

For the Manifold use the blue dun, iron-blue, olive dun, cocked-wing yellow dun, alder, and golden earwig. All but the last-named fly should be winged. Grayling will take any of these flies, but it is as well to have a few apple-green duns and some of Fosbrooke's specialities. A very small black gnat is useful when the river is low.

The Mayfly comes upon the Manifold early in June. It was introduced by John Fosbrooke,

who collected a number of caddises from the
Dove some years ago and ' planted ' them in the
Manifold. The experiment was signally successful, for the green drake now appears regularly
in due season, and is much appreciated by the
trout and grayling. This example might be
followed in other localities.

Between Longnor and Brund Mill, where the
hotel water ends, there is not even a hamlet
close to the river. There are, indeed, but few
houses within sight. Below Brund, where there
is a weir and bridge, the Manifold flows on
through green meadows by Warslow and Ecton
Bridge. A mile or two below Wetton the Hamps
joins the Manifold. As it approaches its confluence with the Dove, the Manifold disappears
below the ground, in a ' water swallow,' to
emerge again in the beautiful estate of Ilam Hall.
The last length of the Manifold is described in
the Dovedale chapter of this book. All efforts
to prevent the burrowing propensity of the
Manifold have failed. The river floweth at its
own sweet will, and in one of its vagaries it
chooses to flow underground for some miles.
A similar phenomenon is seen in the Lathkill,
about two miles from its source.

CHAPTER VI

THIS beautiful sheet of water is in North Stafford-shire, about three miles from the little silk town of Leek. It was made as a reservoir to feed a canal by damming up one end of a valley, and collecting the water of sundry small streams. With the exception of this dam there is no suggestion of artificiality about Rudyard Lake. Turning your back upon the dam, you may fancy yourself in Scotland or the Lake Country, for the shores of the mere are broken into pro-montories, bays, and steep banks of rock and fern, and are well clothed with Scotch firs, birches, and brakes of gorse. There is quite enough wildness in the scene to make one forget that this is an artificial lake not far from the Potteries.

Rudyard is being ' developed.' It is now the property of the North Staffordshire Railway

Company, who will find no difficulty in making the place into a favourite holiday resort. Upon public holidays excursion trains, bearing thousands of trippers, draw up one after another at Rudyard Station, and the water is dotted with pleasure-craft, and the banks fairly sprinkled with fishermen. At other times, and especially in late autumn and winter, when the fishing is usually at its best, Rudyard is one of the quietest pools in England, and the angler will find only one or two brethren of his craft upon the shores.

A five minutes' walk from Rudyard Station brings the visitor to the Hotel Rudyard at the bottom end of the lake. This is a comfortable house of the first class, with several bedrooms, and it stands in a remarkably picturesque position below fir-clad hills. Lodgings can also be obtained in the village. The surrounding district is full of beauty ; the scenery of the Churnet Valley below Leek down to Alton Towers is very delightful, and there are wild, shaggy uplands within easy distance of the village. Anglers can soon reach the Dove and the Blythe at Uttoxeter.

The lake is nearly three miles in length, and

in its widest part it is about half a mile across. On the east side, the Churnet Valley Branch of the North Staffordshire Railway skirts the water below heights of about 700 feet, and on the west shore are woods and broken ground, through which runs a footpath. There are no trees or growth to interfere with fishing from the banks. The depth of the lake varies from 2 to 20 feet or more, and the water takes a stain from the sandstone bed, being neither turbid nor clear, but a good colour for bottom-fishing.

Almost every kind of coarse fish swim in this lake. Roach are very abundant, and fish of 1 pound are frequently taken. There are plenty of carp, and no doubt some of them are weighty, but I have not heard of any over $2\frac{1}{2}$ pounds being captured.* Bream can also be taken in warm weather, and there are large shoals of perch. The heaviest perch caught within recent years was one of 2 pounds, and pound perch are fairly common. Roach were taken last year up to $1\frac{1}{2}$ pounds. Pike are also distributed throughout the water. They are caught by trolling a

* A carp, weighing over 14 pounds, was turned in by the North Staffordshire Railway Company in January, 1903. This enormous carp came from Swynnerton, and is said to be about a century old.

natural or artificial bait from a boat, or by live-baiting with float-tackle from the shores. Small pike appear to haunt the east side. A pike of 11½ pounds was captured off the west shore during the autumn of 1904.

I do not give these weights as representing the heaviest fish taken from Rudyard Lake during the past fifty years, but merely as a hint to the angler concerning the sort of catches which he may justly expect to make. No doubt many good fish are caught and not recorded. I have cited captures which can be authenticated. It would be useful if the North Staffordshire Railway Company could keep a register of notable fish taken from Rudyard. No doubt anglers would co-operate in recording their fish to the keeper or some other official.

There is no restriction as to the length of fish which may be retained by fishermen, and a considerable number of under-sized fish are carried away. Unless the water is overstocked this is to be regretted, and I commend the matter to the notice of the management. I think that the minimum scale should be : Pike, 20 inches ; carp, 11 inches ; bream, 10 inches ; perch, 7 inches ; roach, 7 inches. Pike anglers might be permitted to retain six roach per day under the 7 inches limit for live-baiting purposes only.

I am informed by the North Staffordshire Railway Company that they have restocked Rudyard Lake with several thousands of fish from the Caistor Fisheries, including carp, bream, perch, pike, dace, and roach. Before this stocking, the water had a reputation amongst anglers, so that there is now no scarcity of fish of all sorts in Rudyard Lake, and every promise of their increase in the future if large quantities of immature fish are not taken from the water by 'pot-hunting' fishermen. In short, this water should be regarded as excellent for coarse-fishing.

I cannot indicate every hole and corner of the lake where the visitor may hope to bring perch or carp to the net, but I will divulge one or two haunts of fish. On the west side, just above the boat-house below the dam, many big perch have been caught. Sometimes the hungry pope swarm about here, and hardly give the perch a chance ; but there is good water for perch from the dam right up to the sandy bank above the bay. All around this bay is a capital stand for

the roach and carp angler. It is one of the best
points on the west shore for almost any kind of
fish. One fisherman tells me that he took fifty
roach in two hours from this bay during the
summer of 1904.

With a long rod you can command from 3 to
5 feet of water all along this bank from the dam
up to the second boat-house. The bottom is
firm, and mostly clean. This part of the water
is pretty well ground-baited during the summer
and autumn, and there is always the chance of
catching a few big carp and roach. In the winter
it is not quite so easy to find the feeding-
grounds of the roach. Perch may be looked
for close to the dam and inshore during cold
weather.

The east shore can be worked from a boat with
trolling tackle, though pike-fishing is quite
practicable from the bank. Foster's ' kill-devil '
spinner is a good artificial spinning-bait for this
water. No lead is necessary when using the
' kill-devil ' unless the deeper parts of the lake
are fished. Fishermen must bring their live-
baits, or catch them as required.

The charge for day tickets, which must be
obtained at Rudyard Station, is 1s. a day.

Boat charges are about 5s. per day, and 2s. 6d. for half-day.

I think that I have written enough to make clear that the fishing in Rudyard Lake is well worth the attention of anglers.

CHAPTER VII

THE UPPER WYE

'THE river Wye, then,' writes Charles Cotton,
' has its source near unto Buxton, a town some
ten miles from hence, famous for a warm bath,
and which you are to ride through in your way
to Manchester : a black water, too, at the
fountain, but, by the same reason with Dove,
becomes very soon a most delicate, clear river,
and breeds admirable trout and grayling, reputed
by those who, living upon its banks, are partial
to it, the best of any ; and this running down
by Ashford, Bakewell, and Haddon, at a town a
little lower, called' Rowsley, falls into Derwent,
and then loses its name.'

The limpid Wye still ' breeds admirable trout
and grayling,' and has to this day many devotees
of the rod who are ' partial to it.'   Travelling by
the Midland Railway from Monsal Dale to Buxton
one crosses and recrosses this charming river,

which sparkles in its course between the rugged limestone crags of a remarkably picturesque gorge, provides motor power to sundry mills, and presents a series of reaches delightful alike to the eye of the painter and fisherman.

Buxton* used to be a good centre for fishing the upper waters of the Wye, and it may still serve the angler for headquarters. He will, however, have to visit the Manifold at Longnor, or the Dove at Alsop-en-le-Dale, or Thorpe, if his object is trout and grayling fishing. For those who require bracing air, comfort, and plenty of society, Buxton offers every advantage. There is a good train service to Dovedale, and there is trout and coarse-fishing in Comb's Reservoir, elsewhere described in this book.

Buxton is 1,000 feet above sea-level in a hollow of wild uplands. The Wye comes down from the moors, and at one time there were fish in it close to the town. But with the growth of Buxton the town sewage has polluted the river for nearly five miles down. It is lamentable that such a lovely stream should be the receptacle for poison. The beauty of the scenery, when one is well away

* Hotels : Crescent, Shakespeare ; many boarding-houses.

from the town, is unimpaired, and the Wye flows merrily through Ashwood Dale, Wye Dale, and Chee Dale. But the fish have taken leave of its tainted water, and several miles of fine fishing have been lost to the angler. Some day corporations will learn that trout-fishing is a valuable asset, and that the mediæval system of disposing of town garbage by pouring it into streams that often run low in summer must be abandoned for better and more sanitary methods of sewage disposal. Here is a river that would undoubtedly attract a large number of fishermen to Buxton. It was once noted for the number and the weight of its trout. Fish of 2 pounds were common, and good baskets could be made near to the town. This is all past history. The Wye has been prostituted to the service of a drain. In the Report of the Annual Meeting of the Trent Conservators for 1903 it is stated : ' Buxton : Additional works completed ; can't say whether they will be satisfactory.'

Visitors to Buxton requiring tackle or flies for the surrounding streams should call upon Mr. Banks, a practical angler of long experience, who lives in Spring Gardens.

The Wye throughout the greater part of its

course is in ducal hands. In the next chapter I shall describe the open length below Bakewell, which belongs to the Duke of Rutland. The river from Miller's Dale downwards is sublet to five gentlemen, who claim several miles of trout and grayling fishing. Those who desire to explore the Wye in its most charming lengths may walk from Miller's Dale Station (Midland) to Bakewell through Monsal Dale and Ashford. They will wander for most of the way by the side of an ideal trout-stream, and enjoy the ever-varying scenery of the dales.

At Ashford the stream is widened out to a lake, which has been stocked with rainbow trout. This is a part of the estate of the Duke of Devonshire, and the fishing right is rented by Mr. Clifford-Smith. Below Ashford the Wye enters another pretty ravine, and soon emerges into the meadows above Bakewell Bridge.

CHAPTER VIII

THE WYE : BAKEWELL TO ROWSLEY

I suppose that most fishermen are, like the writer, addicted to loitering on bridges. Very much may be learned of the habits of fish by peering from the parapet of a bridge when the stream is bright beneath the rays of the summer sun. Bakewell Bridge invites to fish-gazing. The Wye comes down from a little weir, bounded on one side by the town, and on the other by a mead below Castle Hill, passes under the stone arches of the picturesque old bridge, and spreads out below in a wide shallow. An island, tenanted by water-hens, small birds, and voles, stands almost in the centre of the stream, and beyond are the green fields of Haddon Hall and the wooded ridges towards Chatsworth.

Peep over Bakewell Bridge, and you will see representatives of the three varieties of trout that thrive in these waters. Very bonnie and tempting are some of these learned trout and experienced grayling. They are quite used to the spectacle of a row of human heads peering from the bridge. That light-coloured fish, looking almost as semi-transparent as a live prawn, is one of the Wye 'ghosts.' Why is it he is so white? I assume that this is a case of the adaptation of colour to environment, though it is curious to remark that one of his neighbours is almost as black as a troutlet from a Welsh mountain peat-hole. These weird fish are fairly distributed up and down the river hereabouts. You may often see one or two of the 'ghosts' just above Wye Bridge, near to Haddon Hall. I have never succeeded in catching these or any other sort of ghosts, though it is my ambition to secure a closer inspection of these mysteries.

The black trout to be seen from Bakewell Bridge are almost as dark as tench. Then there are some handsome golden-brown trout of a more familiar hue and species, and several heavy grayling, low down in the water, and looking somewhat listless upon this hot day. This natural aquarium provides a very interesting sight to the angler who has just come down the hill from the railway-station. Mr. Paul Taylor says it is worth while to go to Bakewell only to look at these big fish that live about the bridge. Now, to look is to desire, and the fisherman who marks these fine fish in this lovely river will yearn to try his skill upon them.

The owner of this alluring stream is the Duke of Rutland, who kindly throws open a long stretch for the enjoyment of visitors to the two hostelries at either end of the preserve. The hotel at Bakewell is the well-known Rutland Arms, the resort of many good anglers for years past. The house overlooks the main street of the quiet little town of Bakewell, and it is about three minutes' walk to the bridge. Here you will chance to meet some of the most expert of fly-fishermen—'regular men,' who have fished the Wye all their lives.* They come every year to revisit the scenes of lively encounters with trout and grayling, for the Wye, like the Dove, takes a grip of you when you have spent a day or two upon its banks.

Not even the Dove in its open lengths can vie with this stretch of the crystal Wye for the

* Four tickets daily are granted to each hotel—the Rutland Arms, Bakewell, and the Peacock, Rowsley. In the height of the season visitors should inquire beforehand when a ticket is available at either of the hostelries.

facility which it affords for casting. It is the
pleasantest of all the rivers upon which I have
cast a dry fly. Scarcely anywhere are you
obstructed by overhanging boughs and grown-up
banks. There are runs and pools in delightful
alternation, and slow glides, which are ringed
with the rises of fish upon a warm May evening.
In a word, the water is perfect for fly-fishing.

It would be too much to expect that the trout
of such an accommodating stream are free risers
to the artificial fly. The fish of this length ' take
some catching.' No one will deny this statement.
But let your basket be three brace, or twice that
number, at the end of the day, you will keenly
enjoy the hours spent between Bakewell and
Rowsley. I have accompanied fishermen to this
water who have angled in all sorts of rivers
in many parts of the kingdom, and almost invari-
ably they have exclaimed, ' What a lovely stream
it is to fish !'

You cannot get angry with this siren Wye.
She may be in a tantrum, and refuse to yield
any of her rich store of fish, but you will still
love her, and continue to flatter her with your
attentions. How smiling and bright she is on
a soft day at the latter end of April, when the

duns are dancing down one of her glides, and the trout are quietly and steadily rising along by grand old Haddon Hall! The cuckoo has just arrived, and the swallows are flashing up and down the stream, which shimmers in blue and silver between meads of spring green, where cows are placidly staring at the angler as they graze among the cowslips and cuckoo-flower.

See that workmanlike fisherman, with pads upon his knees, how he stalks up to the cover of a low alder-bush, and gently flicks out his olive dun into the tiny swirl of a rising trout. At the third cast the rod-top bends prettily, there is commotion in the water, and a struggling trout, the gamest of the game, makes a noble fight for the centre of the pool ere he drops in the landing-net — a handsome fish of about ¾ pound, or maybe of 1 pound in weight; there are many such in the river.

Six weeks or so later and the Mayfly is up. The day is one of intermittent sunshine, and the breeze is damp and westerly. At ten o'clock the graceful green drakes begin to appear on yonder length. By twos and threes they come tripping and fluttering and trying high flights in the air. The swallows dart and swoop, and you hear the

plop, plop of hungry trout. It is the beginning
of the ten days of high carnival. Get to work,
on with your drake, and standing or stooping
well back from the margin of the pool, cast into
those rises.

Ye gods, what a splash ! The biggest trout in
the pool rose to your fly, changed his mind after
one swift pluck at it, and went down like a flash
to the depths. Try again ; the water is boiling
with rises. Ah, you have him ! A good trout,
one of the lusty golden fish that haunt this
place. What do you think now of the Wye ? Is
she not a sweet, fickle, fond temptress ?

Again, the month of October, and the sedge
is brown, and the swallows have departed.
Trout are spawning, but grayling are full of the
joy of life, and feeding greedily upon surface-food.
They rise with a splash, leaving two or three
bubbles on the water. Take your bumble, and
cast it deftly among those bubbles. A rise !
Cast again and again. It is not easy to put
down even the Wye grayling when they are
rising in this fashion. Yes, you have him !
The tenth cast proved irresistible. Your fish
is in fine condition, and almost as bonnie as a
trout. For my part, I would as soon eat him

as a trout, and I deny that he is a poor-spirited
fish to catch.

Once more : let us suppose that you have found
the river in half-flood during April or the earlier
part of May. The water is fining down to an
amber tint, and the trout are mostly busy search-
ing for bottom food. Probably you will see very
few rises to-day, for flies appear to be scarce
over the water. Never mind tradition ; put a
couple of small hackle flies on your cast, and I
will promise you sport. Fish near the bank in
the pools, cast upstream off the edges of the
runs, and work all holes, eddies, and likely corners.
By this method I have taken trout up to a pound
from the Wye early in the season. It is possible
that a hide-bound pundit of the dry-fly cult may
affect to sneer at your style of fishing. Take no
heed of him. I assume that you do not wish
to spend your day watching for phantom rises.
You wish to get a trout or two for your pains.

If the slow pools are rippled by a breeze, you
may catch some nice fish with the wet fly, even
when the trout are not rising to natural insects.
But should the trout be in a rising humour, by
all means use the dry fly. If you find a hatch
of flies on a length of the river, do not leave that

length and go ranging the banks. It is quite probable that this is the only length where flies are in evidence at this time of the year. You may rest assured that if two or three trout are rising in this place there are plenty of fish on the watch for surface insects.

The size-limit for trout on the Duke of Rutland's water is 10 inches. You will catch fish of less than that length, but as a rule the Wye trout are of good proportions. There are some big and wily trout in this length, and it is even within the bounds of probability that you may capture a trout of over 2 pounds. Heavier fish than this frequent the water. In the Rutland Estate Office at Bakewell is a fine specimen of a Wye trout weighing 5¼ pounds.

The rule as to the length of grayling is not quite so rigid. Grayling fairly swarm in this stream. Hundreds were netted out a few years ago, in the hope of lessening the struggle for existence among the trout, and yet grayling still thrive and increase here, as they do in the Dove and Manifold. I cannot enter now into the controversy concerning grayling versus trout. If grayling threaten to outnumber trout in a river, it is a mistake to allow a decimation of the trout.

Still, the grayling is a sporting fish, and I have an affection for him.

It is really astonishing to mark the large number of grayling which may sometimes be seen in shoals on the shallow reaches. They lie quite close together, almost motionless, and are often wholly apathetic to any fly that you may present to them. At other times the grayling all seem to be in the deeper pools, and the bubbles of their rises are visible almost everywhere. You may see them flash up to a floating fly, and sink down again out of sight. The trout in the same pool will be noted nearer to the surface of the water. This limpid Wye is one of the best streams known to me for observing the habits of trout and grayling.

We may now traverse the left bank of the Wye from its junction with the Derwent up to Bakewell Bridge. The confluence is close to Rowsley Station,* on the Midland Railway, which is a four hours' journey by fast train from London. This last length of the Wye is private water. Just above the bridge and the mill, about half a

* Hotel : The Peacock (high class). Visitors can fish the Wye hence to Bakewell. Four tickets only available per day.

mile from the junction, is the first field bordering
the Duke of Rutland's preserve. Some broken
runs, rather overgrown with trees, hold fish, but
we soon reach more fishable and delightfully
open water. Just below a footbridge and a weir
is a good pool, and there are many grayling in
the still above the weir. We pass on to more
open reaches and charming bends with rushing
shallows. Some of the slow glides abound with
both trout and grayling, and if the fish are feeding,
it will be some hours before you reach Wye
Bridge, on the main road. Near the bridge
there is a fine run of broken water, and fish may
be found in the pool below. On the right bank,
just below the bridge, the Lathkill, sometimes
called the Dakin, pours into the Wye. You
can fish from either bank, and a fish or two may
be taken just off the outflow of the Lathkill.

The direction in which the wind is blowing, or
the position of the sun, will determine which
bank you will fish from. Haddon Hall is on the
left bank, about half a mile above Wye Bridge.*
This historic mansion should be visited by the
angler.

Close to Haddon Bridge there is an island, and

* Called sometimes Fillyford Bridge.

above it is a renowned stretch of water much
favoured by dry-fly experts. Above this length
are many excellent pools, which I need not
describe in detail. One may be better than
another, but the best pool on the river is where
trout are rising *pro tem.,* and that is the pool to
discover when you are on the riverside. Trout,
and especially grayling, change their haunts
according to the season of the year. As David
Foster, of Ashbourne, used to say : a casual inspection of a stream will give no knowledge of the
fish within its waters. I suppose most fishermen
have observed that trout appear to quest for
lurking-places where flies are wont to be found in
different seasons. Therefore the run where the
trout are likely to rise in April may be deserted
at the end of June.

In some of the shallows of the Wye you will
notice a large number of grayling During the
spawning time they lie inert on the gravel, and
may be seen by the score. Grayling are more
readily observed than trout, and are not so shy.
Sometimes they lie very near to the riverside,
and are not easily scared by a shadow as are their
companions the trout At other times the grayling are in the pools, and it is then that they

rise most freely to the fly. Some of the Wye grayling weigh over a pound, and the proportion of small fish caught is not a large one. You are not much troubled here with the attentions of shoals of little grayling, which prove a trial in certain rivers.

No Sunday fishing is allowed on this preserve, and no night fishing. The use of bait or the minnow is strictly prohibited, and rightly so, for this is a fly-fishing stream. The river has been lately restocked with native trout, reared in the hatcheries of the Marquess of Granby, on the Lathkill stream.

R. Hensbergh, the river-keeper, who lives near Haddon Hall, provides flies for this length of the Wye. They are tied by his father, and the patterns are known as ' killers ' among Wye fishermen. The casts should be fine and the flies rather small for this river.

CHAPTER IX

THE LATHKILL AND BRADFORD

As a survey of the angling streams of Derbyshire and around would be incomplete without more than a mere reference to the Lathkill and Bradford, I propose to write a short description of these famous waters. It must be understood, however, that the fishing in these streams is only open to those favoured anglers who are among the personal friends of the riparian owners and the lessees. Permission to fish is not granted to strangers.

But fishermen who are interested in trout-streams, whether they may fish in them or not, should not fail to walk through the beautiful dales of the Lathkill and the Bradford, and inspect the various artifices which have been designed with the object of improving upon the natural advantages that the rivers possess. Provided that the visitor follows the public footpaths through the dales, there is no restriction upon his exploration of two of the finest trout-streams in England.

The true source of the Lathkill is in a limestone cave about one and a half miles from the village of Monyash, but in dry weather no water will be seen to issue from the rock-springs. A spring on the right bank, just above Cales Dale, which may be described as a tributary valley to Lathkill Dale, is usually active, and from this point the Lathkill has the character of an upland burn. Few trout will be noted in its waters until we reach the mill below Haddon village, on the left bank. Here there is a fishing lodge belonging to Mr. Symington, who owns the angling right down to Conksbury Bridge.

On this length, which is dammed into a series of pools, there is a trout hatchery and all the accessories of a model fishery. The pools reflect the limestone crags and the trees of the rugged banks, and the pellucid stream breaks into white falls at the weirs. Trout may be seen everywhere in this clear water. In autumn it is a pretty sight to watch them leaping up the falls, and on a fine spring day, when the duns are out, the rise makes one's fingers tingle for a rod.

In about a mile we reach Conksbury Bridge on

the Bakewell and Youlgreave Road.   This is the
limit of Mr. Symington's preserve, and here we
bid farewell to the most enchanting scenery in
the course of the Lathkill.

Below the bridge is the Marquess of Granby's
water, which teems with trout, and gives very
excellent sport with the fly.   The footpath is on
the right bank.   We pass a hatchery, and come
to a horseshoe weir, a stone bridge, and the
keeper's lodge.   On the opposite bank is the
Marquess of Granby's fishing pavilion.   Looking
from the bridge, we shall not fail to see several
good trout standing or rising.

A walk of a few minutes brings us to Alport,
a pretty little village at the confluence of the
Bradford and Lathkill.   The Lathkill tumbles
over several little falls, rushes through the road
bridge, and absorbs the waters of the Bradford
in its swift current.   A charming thoroughfare,
known as the Duke's Drive, conducts us by the
Raven's Tor, or Rainstor Rock, up the valley
of the Bradford.   The stream is ducal property,
and strictly preserved, like the Lathkill.   It is
dammed here and there, and we shall see trout
in every run.   The average weight of the fish is
over $\frac{1}{2}$ pound.

A road on the left, above the Raven's Tor, leads
to Harthill Pond, sometimes called ' Spar Lake,'
or the ' Miners' Lake.'   This pool, which is very
deep towards the middle, is fringed at one end
with rushes, where coots breed and waterfowl of
several kinds resort in the winter.   Harthill Pond
is full of trout ; indeed, it may be described as a
' stew.'   It is used as stock-pool by the Marquess
of Granby.   There are trout of 4 or 5 pounds in
weight in this water.   Upon calm summer
evenings the pond is ringed with the rises of
big trout, and I have seen fish taking the natural
fly madly as early as March 8.   The whole lake
is sometimes alive with rising trout.

Returning to the Bradford, we cross a bridge,
and pass below the gray village of Youlgreave,
where the writer has his domicile.   At a stone
footbridge we cross the stream, pass a little white
house, known as the ' Fisherman's Cottage,' and
pursue our way up Bradford Dale.   The village
of Youlgreave, or Youlgrave, straggles along the
steep bank on the opposite side of the stream,
recalling certain Spanish hamlets that I have
seen.   Keep your eyes on the pools, and you
will see some of the finest trout that swim in
Derbyshire waters.   Fish of a pound and heavier

may be counted by the score in the open parts of the weedy dams. Some are remarkably red on the underside, and all are handsome and well spotted. It is like looking into an aquarium.

A ruined mill and a stone bridge mark the end of the Marquess of Granby's preserve on the Lathkill. The three dams above, and a part of the stream that feeds them, are in the fishing right of Miss M. Melland, of Middleton Hall. Here I have spent many pleasant hours and some very exciting moments, for the trout are big, though distinctly wary. The third or top dam is fed by a clear spring called the Wishing Well. Above this dam the Bradford is a mere brook, which one may leap across. I have, however, caught, with the fly, trout of over a pound in the stream.

Retracing our steps to Alport, we may follow the road by the Lathkill, through a narrow valley, down to the next road bridge. This is the lowest point of the Marquess of Granby's preserve. Below the bridge, down to the junction with the Wye, the Bradford belongs to Major McCreagh Thornhill, Stanton Hall. That part of the stream is sometimes called the Dakin River. It is more overgrown than in its upper length, and is stocked with trout of a goodly weight. Grayling occa-sionally ascend a short distance up this stream.

In writing upon these clear and fishful streams Charles Cotton remarks : ' Lathkin is, by many degrees, the purest and most transparent stream that I ever yet saw, either at home or abroad, and it breeds, 'tis said, the reddest and the best trouts in England.'

An idea of the kind of sport enjoyed by the privileged owners of these little rivers may be gained from a passage in ' The Trout,' by the Marquess of Granby, who records that, on June 8, 1897, ' Mr. T. D. Croft and I killed between us sixty-nine trout, of which number he claimed forty-nine. These forty-nine were caught with the Mayfly in a little Derbyshire stream called the Bradford ; the twenty I killed were taken with the ash dun and blue dun on the Lathkill, into which river the Bradford flows.'

CHAPTER X

I WILL admit that the title of this chapter does not sound inviting to the fisherman. There is a popular conception of the cutlery town likening it to a species of seething inferno, surrounded by gruesome wastes of coal ashes. Sheffield, to many persons in the United Kingdom, simply spells smoke and grime. But this is not quite correct. Few cities in England, perhaps none, can compare with Sheffield in the matter of situation amidst wide moors and rolling hills. On all sides the busy town is surrounded by beautiful country; indeed, some of the finest scenery of the North Midlands lies within a few miles of the heart of Sheffield.

This bustling hive is scarcely the place that one would choose for a quiet holiday. Nevertheless, there are villages hard by that have preserved all the beauty and quaintness of rusticity, and there are pools and streams wherein the angler will find a good store of fish. Sheffield can boast of an Anglers' Association numbering no less than 15,000 members. Think of it. Here is combination, here is the unity born of strength ! The patrons of this powerful association include five members of Parliament and a Mayor. It has a president, vice-presidents, committee, secretary, and trustees. Every year this organization issues an imposing ' Year-Book ' of some eighty odd pages, containing angling records, tide-tables, rules, maps, and particulars as to railway fares to various waters.

Space will not allow me to mention all the lengths of well-stocked rivers rented by this big club. Much of the water is in Lincolnshire, in the meres, drains, rivers, and dykes of that well-watered district. The balance-sheet for 1903-1904 shows the enormous expenditure of £5,869 13s. 5½d. The water rents are nearly £200 per annum, and the salaries of officials and keepers amount to over £100, while a very good balance stands over in the treasurer's hands. Such is the large sum that Yorkshire enthusiasts are willing to expend for the pursuit of the recreation of angling. It is certainly an object-lesson in the power of intelligent co-operation.

Almost all the water rented by this association, which is an amalgamation of a large number of large and small fishing clubs, is stocked with coarse fish. The size-limit for pike is 16 inches, perch 6 inches, roach, rudd, and tench 7 inches, dace 6 inches, chub and bream 8 inches, and barbel 12 inches.

In the winter the association arranges for the delivery of lectures upon piscatorial subjects and natural history, and in the summer there is a big match or gala day. In 1903, 960 fishermen competed in the match, and the prize was won by a capture of 5 pounds 14¾ ounces of fish. £150 were distributed in prizes.

The best fishing lengths of the association are within fairly rapid railway journeys from Sheffield. There are many canal swims near the town, which can be fished by payment of 1s. a day. The secretary is Mr. J. R. Walker, 82, Blake Street, Upperthorpe, Sheffield. The rendezvous and headquarters of the club is at the Three Cranes Hotel, Queen Street. Full information will be found in 'The Sheffield Anglers' Association Year-Book.'

We may now make our bow to this highly commendable and powerful association, and inquire into the prospects for fly-fishing in the vicinity of Sheffield. The trout - fishing is restricted almost entirely to the Corporation Reservoir at Damflask, about seven miles from the town. This fine pool holds a large number of native trout. It is fed by the little river Rivelin. The season begins on March 28, and ends on September 30. In March, April, and September the hours for fishing are from 8 a.m. until 8 p.m. During May and August fishing is allowed up to 9 p.m., and in June and July until 10 p.m. Twenty day tickets cost £1 11s. 6d., and a single day ticket 2s. 6d. Sunday fishing is prohibited. All fish caught under 9 inches in length shall be immediately and carefully restored to the reservoir.

Each ticket-holder is entitled to take away six brace of fish per day. One rod only is allowed to each fisherman, and the bait is confined to fly, worms, gentles, wasp-grub, or artificial spinning-bait. The permits can be obtained from Mr. William Terrey, Waterworks Office, Town Hall, Sheffield.

A trout of 2 pounds, which adorns the window of Messrs. Wood and Company's fishing-tackle shop in Pinstone Street, is, I believe, the record fish from the Damflask Reservoir. Fish of 1½ pounds and a good many 1-pound fish are taken now and then. The average weight is about ½ pound. For artificial flies for this water the visitor should consult Messrs. Wood and Co.

There is another sheet of water within access of Sheffield. This is the Doncaster Corporation Reservoir at Thrybergh. Tickets for a day's fishing are to be obtained at the Mansion House, Doncaster. The water holds trout, and the limit is 10 inches. Fishing opens on March 1, and closes on October 10. Minnows and all artificial spinning-baits are interdicted, except for members of the Corporation. Before July 10 no bait-fishing with worms, grubs, or gentles is allowed, and at no time is ground-baiting permitted. If required by the water-keeper, every person fishing in the reservoir must show the contents of his basket, and state, after fishing, the number of fish retained. Only one rod may be used at one and the same time.

By the Dore and Chinley line from Sheffield the angler can reach the upper lengths of the Derwent described in the section of this book dealing with that river.

CHAPTER XI

NOTTINGHAM-ON-TRENT

NOTTINGHAM is famous for its lace and its fishermen. This goodly town always impresses the writer as one of the brightest and most cheery of industrial centres. As a rule, the angler wishes to leave bustle and commerce behind him when he starts forth on fishing bent, but Nottingham has peculiar, if not unique, claims upon the fisherman. It is the university of distinguished adepts in the art piscatorial. We have all heard of ' the Nottingham style,' ' Nottingham floats,' and ' Nottingham lobs.' You cannot walk for a few yards from the handsome Midland railway-station without realizing that Nottingham folk are as keen upon fishing as upon commerce. Tackle-makers abound, and almost every other inn is the headquarters of a fishing club. If you want to talk ' fish ' with the illuminati, go to cheerful Nottingham town.

The Notts Anglers' Association numbers 2,000 members, and rents many miles of excellent coarse-fishing water.   Another powerful club is the Wellington, and then there is the Notts Piscatorial Society, to say nothing of smaller clubs, and a host of unattached fishermen.

If you live in or within access of Nottingham, and wish to enjoy the many benefits of organization, I advise you to join one of the big clubs. Daily and short-period tickets are not issued by the three big angling societies.   You must have a season ticket or nothing.   Without venturing to criticise this policy, I may say that clubs in other parts of the country find it advantageous to grant facilities to visiting anglers.   There are, however, some anglers who would willingly pay 30s. or £2 2s. a year for the privilege of an occasional visit to well-stocked waters.   But this is not for the fisherman of very modest means.

Is it, then, useless to visit in the neighbourhood of Nottingham with a view to fishing ?   Certainly not.   There are miles of open water on the Trent, besides canal lengths.   Go to Burton Joyce, and you may fish to your heart's content in free water, or pay twopence a day for the right of angling from one bank of the river Trent.   The

tickets can be obtained at the inns at Burton
Joyce and Radcliff Ferry. On the towing-path
side also, in certain reaches, the fishing is free to
the public. Below Gunthorpe there is a long
stretch of free water.

The fish of the Trent in this district are barbel,
chub, bream, pike, roach, perch, dace, and eels.
Mr. C. Jackson, Piscatorial Depot, Drury Hill,
Nottingham, a practical angler and tackle manu-
facturer of sixty-five years' experience in Trent
fishing, will supply you with any kind of tackle
and bait, and give you the benefit of his extensive
knowledge of the river and its tributaries. To
Mr. Jackson I am indebted for much assistance
in writing these notes on the Trent. In years
past this ardent fisherman has taken as much
as 11 stone of coarse fish from the river in a day's
fishing.

' Is this all past history ?' asks my reader.
No, not quite. There are still as many good
fish in the Trent as ever came out of it, but every
angler will agree with me that even coarse fish
are nowadays becoming almost as wily as trout.
The Trent still yields big baskets. It is closely
preserved and guarded by zealous and sportsman-
like fishermen. In the open lengths there are

plenty of bream, some of them up to 4 pounds in weight, good roach, and big chub, and shoals of dace.   The dace and chub take an artificial fly in the Burton Joyce water.   Wheat is a favourite Trent bait for roach.

For the bream-fishing August is about the best month of the year.   Pike begin to take in August, and they may be legally captured then, but the Notts clubs do not fish for pike until September.

Thirty-five years ago Mr. Jackson could catch a couple of brace of grayling from the Trent, with the fly, before breakfast.   Now and again a solitary grayling comes to hand, but the species is practically extinct, except near the mouth of the Dove. At this point there is still the chance of obtaining a grayling or two with an artificial fly.

I will now disclose an interesting matter concerning the Trent.   Mr. Jackson tells me that in January, 1905 (the year in which I write), an extraordinary quantity of salmon ascended the Trent in the Nottingham district.   Mr. Clements, while spinning for pike, ran a very big salmon, reckoned at over 40 pounds in weight, and brought it to the bank after a severe fight.   The fish was immediately released and returned to the water, as it was then the close season.   This same angler counted, in one day in January, eleven large salmon jumping the weir at Averham. Salmon have always travelled up the Trent in favourable seasons, but such a run as that of 1905 is probably unprecedented, and fishermen will watch with interest for the results during the spring and summer.

The Trent salmon are unfortunately proof against the attractions of a ' butcher ' or ' Jock Scott.' There is probably no single fly known to anglers which has not been offered to these obdurate salmon. Wealthy riparian owners have tried their shrewdest arts to tempt the salmon of this river with the fly, but in this matter the power of wealth has failed to triumph over the wisdom of fish. It is good for the rich man that he cannot always have his own way. But the spinning-bait proves dangerous here, and by spinning or bait-fishing only can the Trent salmon be taken.

It seems, then, that 1905 may prove a great salmon year on the Trent. At Shardlow, some years ago, eight salmon were taken by spinning during one day's fishing.

The Grantham Canal, which flows through Lord Manver's estate, can be fished with day tickets issued by the keeper, Coleman. This water contains chub, perch, pike, bream, and eels. At other places along the canal-side fishing leave may be obtained from the farmers. Near Belvoir the Grantham Canal is rented by the Bottisford Fishing Association, which issues daily tickets.

There is excellent trout-fishing at no great distance from Nottingham, though most of it is in private hands. The Dover Beck, near Oxton, holds some big trout, up to 5 pounds in weight, and the water has been well stocked by a riparian owner. There are also large chub and plenty of dace in this stream. Now and again there is the opportunity for acquiring a length on this river from the occupants of small freeholds. A day's fishing in some stretches may sometimes be obtained by an introduction to land-owners.

Another, and perhaps better, trout-stream is the Greet at Southwell, which is well preserved by an angling society. I understand that a day's fishing is occasionally obtainable on some stretches of the Greet, through the favour of owners. This tributary unites with the Trent at Fiskerton.

The Trent is usually rated the best river of England for coarse-fishing. It is certainly an angler's river, abounding with many kinds of fish, and providing recreation for thousands of all classes. Izaak Walton states that the river is 'so called from thirty kind of fishes that are found in it, or for that it receiveth thirty lesser rivers.' It is, however, very doubtful whether the Trent ever bred as many as thirty kinds of fish. Perhaps twenty would be nearer the truth. This theory as to the derivation of the name Trent must have originated very early. Spenser, in the 'Faerie Queene,' writes :

'And bounteous Trent, that in himselfe enseames
  Both thirty sorts of fish and thirty sundry streames.'

Charles Cotton also alludes to the origin of the naming of the river, although he does not lean to one supposition or another. 'Be it how it will,' he writes, 'it is doubtless one of the finest rivers in the world, and the most abounding with excellent salmon, and all sorts of delicate fish.'

CHAPTER XII

THE DERWENT : FROM THE SOURCE TO
GRINDLEFORD

THIS is the chief river of Derbyshire, and from its fountain to its junction with the Trent it is the main artery of the county. Rising in the desolate moors to the north of Ashopton, the Derwent forms the boundary between Yorkshire and Derbyshire for a few miles of its course. At Hathersage the river flows almost through the centre of Derbyshire, and, with a slight trend to the east, it pursues its way to the south through Baslow, Chatsworth, Rowsley, Matlock, Cromford, Belper, Duffield, and Derby to the Trent.

In its higher waters the Derwent receives a number of hill tributaries, and soon becomes a wide stream, with deep pools here and there. The Westend Stream, the Abbey Brook, the Ashop, and the Noe, all contribute to swell its current before the main river reaches the little town of

Hathersage. Below this point the Derwent is joined by Highlow Brook and Burbage Brook. In rainy weather these upper waters are soon tinged with a peat stain from the moors, and this colour is often perceptible as far down as Rowsley. At this point the crystal streams from the limestone region, the Wye, the Lathkill, and the Bradford, mingle their united flood with the Derwent.

With the exception of a few brooks there is no tributary of importance below Rowsley until we reach the junction of the Amber at Ambergate. Lower down, on the right bank, the Ecclesbourn Brook flows in at Duffield. Below Derby there is no subsidiary stream of any size.

Derbyshire folk of the passing generation call the river 'the Darrent water.' There is little doubt that the name of the stream is derived from the ancient British *dwr*, water, and *wen*, white. In summer the Derwent is a 'white water,' except in times of spate, so that the appellation is fairly correct. But the river is never quite so translucent as the limestone streams of the country.

There are few reaches on the Derwent, above Belper, which can be described as uninteresting from the scenic point of view, and there are none without their store of trout and grayling. The lower reaches of the river through Darley Dale, above Matlock, have perhaps the least charm of any length until we approach Derby, but these ' flats ' are not devoid of quiet, pastoral features.

In its more mountainous course from the source to Ashopton, the river has several small cascades, and affords a beautiful facsimile of a Scotch upland burn. Lower down the Derwent flows in a deep vale, with imposing and well-wooded slopes, and at Chatsworth art has perhaps added to the natural beauty of the stream.

The Matlock gorge is remarkable ; the limestone cliffs rise sheer above the water, and the river hurries and tumbles in its confined and rocky channel. Thence, down to the town of Belper, the Derwent alternately glides and meanders dreamily amid less wild but picturesque surroundings of wooded ridges and green meadows. At Derby the river is turbid and unlovely.

James Croston, who wrote an interesting account of a journey, ' On Foot through the Peak,' in 1862, says, concerning the scenery of this river : ' Though not possessing those features of wild desolation and stern sublimity which characterize and give interest to the Dove, the Derwent may nevertheless challenge comparison with any river in the kingdom for the rich and varied character of the scenery throughout its course. Generally its banks are well wooded ; the stately oak, the towering elm, and the wide-spreading sycamore, mingling their rich verdure with the more light and graceful foliage of the tall ash or silvery birch.'

Charles Cotton alludes once or twice to the Derwent, and calls it ' a black water.' I have shown that the Derwent is liable to deeper discoloration than the limestone rivers of the district, but it is scarcely a ' black water ' under normal conditions. As a rule, the river is quite clear, and, in fact, almost too clear, during the greater part of the season. Cotton is, therefore, incorrect in his statement that the stream is darkly stained ' quite through its progress.' Rising in a humid and hilly region, the Derwent is subject to floods, which sometimes overflow the banks and submerge the low-lying fields. In high spate the river floods the racecourse and environs of Derby. It would be a fairer description to say that the Derwent is a brown water after heavy rain and a clear one in dry weather.

At the end of Derwent Dale, the first of the dales, with an appellation, watered by the

'Darrent,' the Ashop Stream flows in on the left bank. The Ashop has two forks, one rising on Glossop Moor and running down Ashop Clough ; the other flowing down from Alport Moor. These brooks unite near the Snake Inn on the elevated road between Sheffield and Glossop.

We are here in the very heart of the High Peak. Kinder-Scout, which rises to a height of 1,981 feet, is reared among the lonely uplands to the south-west of the inn. The Snake itself stands over 1,000 feet above the sea-level, in a region of wind-swept grouse-moors, bogs, and deep ravines Glossop, a busy little town, lies seven miles away to the north-west, and marks the confine of modern civilization.

This is an ideal resting-place for the town-weary fisherman, who loves moorland scenery and the company of a prattling hill-stream. Sheffield, about seventeen miles away, lies at the other extremity of this wild tract of country, and is the postal town. In the winter letters are only delivered at this mountain hospice upon three days in the week. Here is real seclusion, rugged, impressive scenery, and bracing air, with good brook-trouting to boot.

The Snake Inn, in spite of its remoteness,

provides well for guests. There are six miles of trout-fishing for a guinea per season or half a crown a day. Bait-fishing is allowed, as well as the artificial fly. Up to August 10 there are eight bedrooms to let, but after that date the house is usually full of grouse-shooters. Terms are quoted as ' moderate.'

Close to the village of Ashopton, on the Derwent, the Ashop runs into the main river on the right bank, while the Lady Bower Brook flows in a little lower down on the left bank. The highroad is here carried across the Derwent. Ashopton is a diminutive village amidst heath-clad hills, the principal height being Win Hill, whence there is a remarkably fine and wild view.

The river and brook fishing hereabouts is attractive, and the Ashopton Inn caters well for anglers. The inn is now one of the ' model public-houses ' under the direction of the People's Refreshment House Association, whose president is the Bishop of Chester. Having experienced, from time to time, considerable trouble in obtaining reasonable refreshment other than beer and spirits at licensed houses in various parts of the kingdom, I hail the scheme with pleasure. There are occasions when a cup of tea is more enjoyable than a glass of ale,

or when one wishes for a light meal. How often,
in spite of the law, have I been refused victuals by
licensed *victuallers* ! I trust that we shall soon
have an end of this abuse of houses of entertainment by license-holders. The insane conserva-
tism of the innkeeper who refuses a customer food
is incomprehensible.

At the Ashopton Inn you will find a good cook,
decent meals, and a bath-room with hot water.
There are seven bedrooms, and plenty of stabling.
Three miles of trout-water are open to visitors at
half a crown a day, with a reduction to guests
staying in the house. Bait-fishing is allowed.
The nearest station is Bamford, and vehicles will
be sent to meet any train, if notice is given to the
Manager, Ashopton Inn, Derwent, which is the
postal and telegraphic address.

May and June is a favourite time for trout-
fishing in these higher reaches and tributaries of
the Derwent. The casts should be fine and the
flies dressed rather small.

About half a mile below Ashopton the Lady
Bower Brook flows into the Derwent on the left
bank. This is a charming little rivulet, running
down a delightful dale. It contains a fair number
of trout, and has one open length in its course.

This is at the Lady Bower Inn, beautifully placed on the highroad from Sheffield, which is about ten miles distant. The highway descends from a height of over 1,100 feet to the dell of the Lady Bower Brook, which it crosses at Cut-throat Bridge before reaching the inn.

There are two bedrooms to let at the inn, and the fishing is free to visitors for about a quarter of a mile. Worm-fishing is allowed. The surrounding scenery is very typical of the wilder parts of the Peak Country. About two miles from Bamford, in a lonely and beautiful part of the Peak District, is the old hostelry of the Yorkshire Bridge Inn. The proprietor, P. Bradley, owns the fishing right for three quarters of a mile of the Derwent. There are three bedrooms and two sitting-rooms at the inn. The cost of a season ticket for this length is £1. Day tickets are issued at 2s.

Two fields above Yorkshire Bridge, below Ashopton, is the upper limit of the Derwent Fly-fishers' Club length, which is continued on one side of the river, in certain parts, down to Newbridge, and nearly to Calver Weir, above Baslow. This club rents about ten miles of water. Membership is limited to twenty rods. The entrance-fee is £10 10s., and the yearly subscription

£10 10s. The Derwent Fly-fishers have their own
trout hatchery, and they also purchase trout for
turning in from other trout farms.   This beautiful
stretch of the Derwent is well stocked, and the
average weight of the trout is three to the pound.
Grayling are abundant, and run a little larger on
the average.

The season here for trout begins on April 1, and
closes on October 1.   Grayling afford best sport
in the autumn.   Most of the members fish habitu-
ally with the dry fly.   The secretary is Mr.
Herbert Barber, Dore, near Sheffield.   T. Outram,
the water-bailiff, lives at Grindleford village.
There is a new and comfortable hotel near the
railway-station, and also the Commercial in the
village, one mile from the station.   The surroundings of Grindleford are delightfully picturesque,
the heights being clad on their lower slopes with
Scotch firs and birches.   There is a fine view of the
Derwent Valley from the village, which stands
high above the right bank of the river.

We will now retrace our steps up-stream from
Grindleford.   About two miles below Yorkshire
Bridge is the village of Bamford, a little wide of
the Derwent.   The river is broader here, and there
are many good runs for trout and grayling.   Here,

as in the district generally, the scenery is charming, and the sense of isolation from the crowd complete. By shifting from one inn to another the roving angler can enjoy some pleasant days by these brawling streams, and fish with either the dry or wet fly. Nor is he debarred from the use of the worm and minnow.

At Bamford there is a large hotel, with twelve bedrooms, called the Marquis of Granby. The proprietor has the fishing right over one mile of the Derwent, and the length is noted for trout and grayling. Half a crown a day is the charge for fishing.

At Mytham Bridge, about a mile below Bamford, the little river Noe or Now joins the Derwent on the right bank. This tributary, which flows through charming country, rises on the slopes of Kinder Scout, the chief height of the group of hills forming the Peak of Derbyshire. Flowing through the quiet Vale of Edale, the Noe passes the village of Hope, where it is joined by a rivulet known as Peaks Hole Water, which comes down from the hills above Castleton. Lower down, on the right bank, another stream flows into the Noe. This is the Bradwell Brook, which rises close to the village whence it derives its name.

A third tributary of the Noe joins that stream close to its confluence with the Derwent at Mytham, and it waters the secluded valley called Otter Dale. The Noe is a good trout and grayling stream, but it is not open to the visiting angler, unless he has the privilege of belonging to the club of six members owning the fishing rights. The society is known as the Peak Forest Angling Club, and the secretary is Mr. P. Rhodes, who resides at Rotherham. A rather high rent is paid for the water, which extends from Edale to Mytham Bridge on the Derwent, and includes lengths on the Peaks Hole Water and Bradwell Brook. The water-bailiff to the club is George Ashton, who lives on the riverside, close to Hope. He is an experienced fisherman and a fly-tier.

Hathersage, a small town, is on the left bank of the Derwent, about three miles down from Mytham Bridge. The fishing for a length here is in the right of Colonel Shuttleworth, of Hathersage Hall, to whom inquiries should be addressed.

CHAPTER XIII

THE DERWENT : THE CHATSWORTH FISHERY

WE have now reached a very attractive and well-stocked length of the Derwent. The chief riparian owner hereabouts is the Duke of Devonshire, and the water is preserved by an influential club of fishermen, numbering twenty-five members, who pay an entrance-fee of £5 5s. and a yearly subscription of a like amount.

Let us first make our survey of this fishery, starting from the termination of the Derwent Fly-fishers' Club water at Newbridge Weir. The valley of the river winds below Curbar Edge and the high grouse-lands of East Moor, dividing the region of heather from the limestone hills of Stoney Middleton and Calver. Streams and pools alternate, and in a mile or so we reach Calver, a little village with an inn and bridge. The weir here is a good spot for trout, and the water, varying in its character from run to still, is adapted for both wet and dry fly fishing.

The next village below is picturesque Baslow, with the Rutland Arms Hotel on the left bank, close to the bridge. Above the bridge is a weir, and above the weir is a stretch of quiet water, which holds many good trout and grayling. This is a favourable pool for dapping with the natural fly in the summer, or for dry-fly fishing in the evening. Below the bridge at Baslow the Derwent spreads out into a number of pretty runs, offering water for the wader, which should keep him well employed during a rise of trout.

Baslow has several hotels and a hydropathic establishment. It nestles below the moors, and has an air of prosperity and comfort in its hostelries and solid stone cottages. For the Chatsworth length this is the best place for headquarters, as the village is practically in the middle of the preserve. Travellers from the North may book to Grindleford Station, and drive hence to Baslow, while those coming from the South may alight at Bakewell, and proceed hither by carriage.

Soon after passing through Baslow Bridge, the river enters Chatsworth Park. On the right bank

is Edensor village, and on the left the imposing
mansion of the Cavendish family, with its fine
gardens, conservatories, fountains, and sheet of
ornamental water. An ornate bridge spans the
river here, and below there are several artificial
dams across the stream, which have been constructed for the benefit of the fly-fishermen.

The Derwent leaves Chatsworth Park beneath
another bridge, and flows on to Beeley, where the
mill-stream is full of trout. About two miles below
Beeley we come in sight of Rowsley Bridge, where
the Chatsworth Fishery ends and the Darley Dale
Club length begins.

The beautiful stretch of water which we have
hurriedly traversed may be said to provide the
finest trout-fishing in the whole course of the
Derwent.   It offers in its nine miles an abundance
of pools and broken streams, and it is also well
supplied with tributaries.   A water so diverse in
character can be fished in some parts from the
banks, and in others by wading.   If the pools are
the object of attack, deep wading is necessary
in certain places, but ordinary thigh-wading
stockings will serve as a rule.   The fisherman who
wades up-stream, and fishes with a couple of wet
flies, will find many runs to his liking ; while the

votary of the dry fly will not seek far for water in which he may note rising trout and grayling.

I will here describe the conditions upon which visiting anglers can obtain fishing for trout and grayling in this portion of the Derwent. Although this is a club water, the visitor is not debarred from angling. Temporary residence at the Rutland Arms, or the Peacock at Baslow, or at the Chatsworth Hotel, Edensor, entitles the stranger to fish in the preserve. The day fisherman, who is not a guest at these hotels, can buy a ticket for 3s. It is, however, necessary to note that these day tickets are limited in number.*

During the past sixteen years this length has been restocked annually. In 1903, 10,000 trout fry were turned into the tributaries. In 1904 3,000 yearling Loch Leven trout were distributed in the main river ; and in February, 1905, 5,000 more Loch Levens were purchased for restocking. Besides this replenishing from year to year, the brooks are periodically netted, and the fish conveyed to the river. Five hundred brace of

* The following hotels have each season a limited number of day tickets for non-resident fishermen: Rutland Arms, 40; Peacock, 40; Wheatsheaf, 15; Chequers, 15; Baslow Hydro, 15; and the Chatsworth Hotel, Edensor, 15.

takeable fish were returned from the tributaries in 1904. This restoration of trout from the brooks lessens very greatly the risk of damage by poaching, and tends to keep up a plentiful supply of fish in the main stream. These affluents produce a large number of trout.

The fishery is fairly free from predatory fish. There are a few chub, and one has been taken with the fly, weighing 3 pounds. Dace are to be found here and there, and also some barbel. The water is entirely free from pike. Travelling otters occasionally visit the water, and a few have been trapped during the past twenty years ; but Bacon, the head-keeper, informs me that there are no holts on the preserve, and that otters do not lie up in this part of the Derwent.

' How many brace of trout may a fairly good angler expect to catch here in a day's fishing ?' is a query that I anticipate from the reader. Such a question is never easy to answer without a knowledge of the interrogator's capability with the rod. Much depends also upon the time of the year, and the state of the weather and the water. I will, however, set down some ' takes ' made in the fishery by expert fishermen.

Mr. Moon, a member of the club, caught in one

day with the fly, in May, sixteen brace of trout and seven brace of grayling. The grayling, being out of season, were returned to the water, and so were some of the trout, being undersized. This angler has occasionally averaged ten to eleven brace of fish per day during a visit to Baslow. Another angler, Mr. Brookes, fishing with the fly after a thunder-shower, captured twelve brace of trout and grayling in one short length of the river. Some of the fish were $\frac{3}{4}$ pound, and none weighed less than $\frac{1}{2}$ pound.

Mr. Thompson, a visitor, fishing below Chatsworth late in the season, caught on the first day of his visit ten and a half brace ; on the second day, thirteen and a half brace ; and on the third day, ten brace. Mr. Pitt, the station-master of Rowsley, has taken eight and a half brace of fish in a day from this water. These are the occasional records of adepts, and they may be repeated or even bettered by experienced fly-fishermen. But it would be rash to *promise* such sport to anyone who visits the Chatsworth Fishery. Three to six brace may be said to be the kind of basket which rewards the less skilful and sagacious anglers in this water. However, all generalizations are risky, and I now quit the dangerous topic with the remark that there are plenty of fish and very pretty fishing from Newbridge down to Rowsley.

In the spring wet-fly fishing will be found the most profitable method. The middle of May often brings out a show of flies on the water, and trout begin then to rise in earnest to surface insects. Still, taking one year with another, June is a better month for dry-fly fishing in this length. Before May the floating fly is decidedly less alluring than the sunk fly. Therefore in April and May rely chiefly on your two sunk flies, fished up-stream. September often proves a fortunate month on this length. It is then that grayling begin to rise most freely.

There is not a very large hatch of Mayfly here, but sport may be had when the drakes make their appearance. In the still water some good fish may be attracted by fishing with the natural May-fly, or by dapping the blue-bottle. These modes of fishing are allowed by the club. For general use in the Chatsworth water the following flies are recommended : ash dun, olive dun, March brown, claret bumble, furnace bumble, apple green, and black midge. In a coloured water the March brown kills at any period of the season.

The trout in this preserve average a little under

½ pound, but plenty over 1 pound are caught. Grayling are perhaps a trifle heavier as an average.

The secretary of the Chatsworth Club is Mr. C. F. Fieldsend, Edensor, Bakewell. A. Bacon, the chief water-bailiff, lives at Baslow.

Minnow-fishing is entirely prohibited by the club rules, and only members are allowed to fish with the worm. No worm-fishing is permitted until June 1. All undersized fish must be returned to the river.

CHAPTER XIV

THE DERWENT : ROWSLEY TO MATLOCK

THIS length of the Derwent is rented by the Darley Dale Angling Club of thirty members. The club water begins about three quarters of a mile above Rowsley, and ends just above Matlock Bridge Station, covering a distance of nearly eight miles. Fishing is permitted from either bank, and wading is allowed.

To become a member of this club, it is necessary to wait for a vacancy, and to secure a proposer and seconder, who must belong to the association. Members are elected by ballot, and the subscription is £4 4s. a year.

There are certain distinct advantages connected with membership. The whole of the water is open to clubmen ; they have a voice in the management of affairs, and receive annually twenty transferable tickets, which they can give to friends. Twelve of these tickets are for fly-fishing, and eight are for bottom-fishing.   Only members are allowed to fish with the minnow.

Failing to obtain membership, anglers may purchase for £2 per annum a ticket enabling them to fish about half of the length—*i.e.*, from Darley Bridge to Matlock.   The secretary may use his discretion in the granting of these season tickets.   The visiting fisherman, whose leisure is scanty, can fish, with artificial fly, the whole length (about four miles) of this water for 2s. 6d. a day.   These day tickets can be purchased at the Square and Compass Inn, Darley Bridge, or from the secretary, Mr. J. H. Dawson, Darley Dale, near Matlock.   The season for trout opens on March 25, and ends October 1 ; and for grayling the close season is from March 15 to June 15. The size-limit for fish is 9 inches.   Season and daily ticket-holders must not fish before 6 a.m. nor after 9 p.m.   There are two bailiffs upon the length.   One of them, Allen of Rowsley, is a good fly-dresser.

Such are the essential points in the rules issued by the Darley Dale Angling Club.   I will now conduct the fisherman to the water, starting from Rowsley Bridge, and give him such counsel as I may be entitled to offer from my own experience of two seasons on this length, together with valuable information kindly supplied by members of the club.

Below Rowsley Bridge is a large and deep pool, breaking at the tail end into two streams, parted by an island of pebbles and bushes. Assuming that the stranger is provided with wading-stockings, let him enter the water from the right bank, and try his dry fly over the fish which one rarely fails to see rising in this pool. I have had both trout and grayling from the pool, and also from the runs below. On a summer evening, from 7 till 9, the fisherman may often note a number of good fish on the feed off the right bank of the bridge-pool ; and I am convinced that there are two or three heavy trout in this corner, besides a large number of trout and grayling of over ½ pound. In a stained water, I have taken fish here with the wet fly.

Below the tumbling run is a rather long still, which yields a fish or two occasionally, and at the outflow of the Wye is another double stream and an island. These runs are always likely, and at times fine grayling may be taken here. Unless the Wye is in high flood, it can be crossed by the wader near its mouth. Following the right bank, we reach a straight, rather deep stretch, containing a fair number of fish, especially at the lower end. The next run is a strong one, and in the pool above it are some heavy grayling, while the run itself usually affords a trout or two.

Lower down bushes somewhat obstruct the fly-fisherman for a short length ; but it is well to watch this part for rises, as it is a quiet harbourage for fish. Above the next bend, where the river is broken into several tumbling runs, is a deep pool which fishes well at most times. It is always worth while to watch this pool, especially in the evening. Flies seem to favour this length, and there is often a good rise along the right bank and at the tail of the pool, just off a steep clay bank.

Stanton Wood House, a shooting lodge of the Marquess of Granby, is among the trees on the right bank. There is a seat under a big tree, and the wide pool below should not be passed by. A shallow lower down can be crossed when the water is low, and it is as well to make for the left bank of the river, as the right bank is overgrown and high almost all the way down to Darley Bridge.

The water from Stanton Wood House to the bridge is varied in character, and has one or two long deeps, where fish may often be seen on the rise. There are also some runs which will tempt the wet-fly fisherman after a freshet in the river. Only a small number of anglers hereabouts use the wet fly, but I know, from my own experience, that it is effective early in the season and at dusk in summer time. But, as a rule, it is better worth one's time to mark rising or standing fish, and throw a dry-fly over them.

Having reached Darley Bridge, it is a matter of comparative unimportance whether the angler elects to follow the right or the left bank. There is some streamy water for about a quarter of a mile, and then a pool, which is best fished from the sandy left bank. There is a fording place at the tail of this pool, where a little green island and a big sunken tree will be noted. Good trout and grayling feed under the alders on the right bank, and by wading in a yard or two from the left bank you can reach them. I have seen this pool fairly ringed with rises on a warm evening in June, just upon dark.

Cross again to the right bank, and try down the runs and the long, straight, slow pool below it. At a bend, where the river narrows, and a brook flows in on the left bank, there is a likely stand for both trout and grayling. The latter often feed off the outlet of the brook in winter.

There is a long scour lower down, flowing into another of the characteristic deep pools. This pool is favoured by bottom-anglers, who fish here for trout and grayling with float tackle. Below, where the railway touches the left bank, there is a double run and an island. The tail of these streams should be watched for rising fish, and there is good fly-water down to the next bend. Grayling are perhaps more abundant in the next deep than in any other reach of the club water. It is a bad day indeed when fish are not rising in this length. There are some big grayling here, especially under the boughs on the left bank, and in Mayfly time this is an excellent stand for trout. The water is too deep for wading, except at the top of the pool, where there is a firm gravel bottom.

We now come to Oaker Bends, below Oaker Hill, made immortal by Wordsworth in a poem upon the two brothers who planted the tree on the summit. These sharps contain trout, and they are best fished with the wet fly. Below them are several deep pools succeeding each other down to the railway bridge just above Matlock.

The Derwent is not an ' early ' river in this
valley, therefore it is as well to postpone fly-
fishing until the middle or end of April, unless
that month is especially mild.   There are days in
early spring when you may enjoy a few hours'
sport by fishing with two or three small hackle
flies in the tails of the runs.   But this is a snowy
country, and winter sometimes lingers on till May.

May and June are good months for the dry fly,
and later on in the season, during hot weather,
there is usually a fair evening rise of trout and
grayling in most of the pools which I have
mentioned.   October is the best time for grayling.

There are fortunately very few predatory fish
in this length.   Some heavy barbel haunt some
of the deeps and eddies, but they are very rarely
fished for.   I think that the barbel fisherman
might have sport here if he baited two or three
swims.   The parts where I have noted big barbel
are in the tail of the pool below Rowsley Bridge,
in the slow water above Darley Bridge, and in the
pool below, and also at the top of the pool above
Oaker Bends.   A barbel of 7 or 8 pounds brushed
against my leg one evening while I was wading
near the right bank at the bottom of Rowsley

Bridge Pool.   I have also noted big barbel just above Matlock Bridge.

Among the Darley Dale Clubmen there are some very keen and clever dry-fly anglers, as well as two or three ladies, the wives of members. There is no bottom-fishing allowed in the upper water above Darley Bridge, and the minnow is rarely used in the club water.

The trout-flies most generally favoured on this preserve are the gravel-bed, green drake, red-spinner, iron-blue, yellow dun, and claret bumble. For grayling try the fiery bumble, apple-green dun, red-tag, and Foster Brothers' specialities for Derbyshire rivers.   The yellow dun, dressed by Eaton of Matlock, is a good summer fly, and should be used during a late evening rise.

While these pages were passing through the press, I learned that one club is turning in several hundreds of trout this season, 1905.

CHAPTER XV

THE DERWENT : FISHING AROUND MATLOCK

FOLLOWING the course of the Derwent down from the boundary of the Darley Dale Club water, we reach a short length of free fishing at Matlock Bridge. 'The Matlocks' are three overgrown villages, known to-day as Matlock Bank, Matlock Bridge, and Matlock Bath. On the Bank are the principal hydropathic establishments, with Smedley's dominating all of them. The Bridge part of the Matlocks has a street of shops, and two or three hotels close to the river. In about a mile, following the Derwent by the imposing High Tor, we enter Matlock Bath, where there are hotels, boarding-houses, pleasure-grounds, and another thoroughfare of shops.

Matlock is a convenient centre for the fisherman. It has two stations on the Midland main line, which, from Derby to beyond Miller's Dale, runs first in the valley of the Derwent, and afterwards follows the course of the Wye.   There is accommodation to suit all pockets in the Matlocks, and the fishing is of a varied character.   From Matlock Bridge downwards the Derwent contains very big trout.   For heavy fish of this species, throughout the course of the Derwent, there is perhaps no better length than this.

The record trout, taken with the fly, was captured by Mr. J. G. Eaton, the local fly-tier and angling correspondent.   It weighed 6 pounds 2 ounces, and was killed near the iron footbridge below Matlock Bridge in the free water.   Heavier trout than this have been caught at Matlock with bait.   During last season (1904) the expert Mr. Eaton captured four handsome trout from this water.   The heaviest scaled 4½ pounds, and the smallest 2¾ pounds.   The biggest was taken on a yellow dun.

These big trout at Matlock are not simpletons. They are fairly harried by anglers throughout the season.   Notwithstanding, the score of large trout taken at Matlock every year is a high one, and it is no exaggeration to say that trout of 2 and 3 pounds are plentiful in the deep pools of this length.   The monsters usually rise to fly about dusk, and if the fisherman is on the spot at the right time, he stands a fair chance of securing one or two fine trout in an evening's fishing.

The Derwent tumbles through Matlock Bridge in a strong stream, forming a capital run below. At the iron bridge its course is slow, and the water is deep for some distance. Big trout may be seen rising here on any warm evening in the summer, and there are also grayling and coarse fish in these deeps. The biggest grayling from this water was taken by Mr. Eaton's father, fishing with a worm. It weighed 2¾ pounds.

Most fishermen will wish to go a little further from the town reach at Matlock, and a day ticket, obtainable for 1s. from Mr. Hartley, near the tramway terminus, will give them license to fish with bait or fly nearly down to Cromford. Below this the charge is 2s. for the day, and the artificial fly only is allowed.

This length is preserved by the Matlock and Cromford Angling Club. A considerable part of the water is deep, and some stretches have wooded and steep banks. But, by hook or by crook, the fisherman should endeavour to fish these long, deep, overgrown pools, for they abound with good trout and grayling. Here and there one finds an excellent run of broken water, where the fly can be used with effect early in the summer, or at twilight in July and August.

Bottom-fishermen, whether they pursue trout, grayling, or roach, will find many likely corners and deep holes in this part of the Derwent. Below the High Tor, on the left bank, is a big weir, and the streams below it are favourite haunts of trout. The natural minnow, on a spinning flight, is an attractive bait in these rough streams.

At Matlock Bath the river is wider and more placid in its flow. In the summer this reach is much disturbed by boats, but it contains big trout, and abounds with roach. There are also pike, perch, and barbel in this length, but they are more abundant below Cromford and at What-standwell, where the coarse-fishing is well worth attention.

There are many other attractions besides fishing at Matlock, but of these I need not speak here, as they are more correctly in the province of a book for the general tourist. I may say, however, that there is a wealth of fine scenery in and around each of the Matlocks, and that the place is well situated for excursions to many charming and interesting places in the High Peak District.

Before we proceed further down the Derwent,

I will draw the trout-fisherman's attention to three dams in the neighbourhood of Matlock Bridge. These pools are at Tansley, under two miles from Matlock Bridge Station. They are owned by the proprietor of a large mill, who issues day tickets at 2s. 6d. The upper dam is about an acre in extent, and contains some good trout, but it is rather too overgrown for fly-fishing, and the water is apt to sink in hot weather. There is a better depth of water in the larger dam below it, the pool that we first see upon leaving the mill. The banks are fairly open, and the water can be fished with the fly. By wading you can command almost the whole pool.

I have caught some fair trout here, but nothing remarkable in the way of weight, though I am told that there are heavy fish in these dams.

The third dam is the prettiest of the group. It is surrounded by trees, and it is almost impossible to fish it without wading, except at the sluice end. This pond literally swarms with small trout of about 3 ounces or ¼ pound, which rise freely enough to a wet fly on a dull, windy day. I have caught fish here with the dry fly during a rise to the naturals. A good point is from the bank near the sluice. At the upper end of this dam is

9

a shallow, where a brook enters, and this is a favourite feeding-place for trout.

These pools are worth trying with the fly on a breezy day in May or June. Bottom-fishing is permitted.

There are two more dams at Two Dales, very prettily situated with woody and rocky banks. They are private, and rented by that good angler, Dr. S. Warneford, of Two Dales. There are a fair number of trout in these pools, up to 1 pound in weight, but the average is lighter. The fish are not very free risers to the artificial fly, though they can be taken with the sunk fly about dusk and on dull, windy days.

The lower length of the Matlock and Cromford Angling Club water is better stocked and more easily fishable than the upper length. It begins at Cromford Bridge, with a good streamy flat, which can be waded. The railway crosses the river just below, and from the rail-bridge downwards for about half a mile the water is deeper and broken, and has several fine pools. Further down, where the Derwent bends to the railway, there is a noted run for trout and grayling, and good wading water.

After the middle of May this water yields the

best baskets to the dry-fly anglers, but before then the wet fly may be used with advantage. Eaton of Matlock dresses flies for this water, and can direct visitors to the likeliest runs for trout and grayling. The fish here do not attain the weight of the well-fed trout and grayling of the Matlock deeps, but they are more abundant, and less worried by anglers.

In this preserve bait-fishing is allowed from Cawdor Bridge to the Collingwood stream. Below that point the artificial fly is only permitted. The Cromford length contains some heavy barbel, but the coarse-fishing is reserved for members only. Barbel-fishing is not pursued here as a fine art, as in the Thames and Trent. Nevertheless, good sport awaits those who care to bait a swim.

During about two hours' fishing in the month of September 175 pounds of barbel have been taken from this length. The heaviest fish weighed $9\frac{3}{4}$ pounds. This catch was made in water 3 feet in depth, and the bait was the tail of a lob-worm. Barbel of over 7 pounds are not uncommon in this part of the Derwent.

From Leawood Deeps down to Ambergate the Derwent holds some of the biggest perch to be found in any river of the United Kingdom.

Perch from 2½ pounds to 3½ pounds have been taken here, and in one day's fishing, some years ago, a baited swim afforded over 1 hundred-weight of perch. Minnows will prove an attractive lure for these big perch, which may be collected together by a liberal ground-baiting of worms. I cannot promise a successful day with the perch, if they are sought for without discrimination. The water must be studied and the haunts of perch discovered before the ground-bait is thrown in. A little trouble in the selection of two or three holes and corners will repay the fisherman, for the perch hereabouts are remarkably heavy, and give excellent sport.

Below the limit of the club water is a private preserve, known as the Homesford Cottage water, which is free to visitors at this house of entertainment. The length is noted for grayling, and contains a fair number of trout. There is good coarse-fishing here for perch, roach, and barbel, with the chance of taking pike. Although war is waged against pike in the club length, a moderate number of these enemies to trout survive and breed. Homesford Cottage is about a mile from Whatstandwell Station, on the road from Derby to Buxton.

CHAPTER XVI

THE DERWENT : WHATSTANDWELL TO DERBY

ALTHOUGH we have left the finest scenery of the Derwent behind us, the river valley has still much beauty and attractive serenity. The banks, with their background of wooded heights, are typical of the High Peak region, and the stream, though less impetuous in its course, is varied with long deeps and rippled shallows.

Whatstandwell is built on the slope of a steep hill, on the left bank of the river. The village has a station on the Midland main line, and hard by, close to the old stone bridge, is the snug Derwent Hotel,* in the charge of Mr. Mountney, a keen sportsman and good host.

If we have passed the best trout lengths on the Derwent, it may be said that we have reached the beginning of the finest stretch for all-round

* Accommodation for visiting fishermen, and leave to fish in private water.

133

fishing. The water is, however, by no means devoid of trout, and it has some very productive grayling runs. From this village down to Belper the Derwent holds some of the biggest trout to be found in its course, though it is not the best of lengths for fly-fishing. For grayling, however, it can hold its own with some of the higher lengths. The coarse-fishing for perch, roach, and barbel is good, and pike are moderately plentiful. Whatstandwell is, therefore, a rendezvous of bait-anglers rather than fly-fishers ; but there is fly-fishing for grayling from the railway-bridge down to the deeps below the road-bridge, a distance of about one and a quarter miles. This stretch is full of grayling, and most parts of it can be fished by wading.

The Derwent Hotel water extends from the railway-bridge on the left bank down to about three-quarters of a mile above Ambergate. The upper part is mostly swift and broken water, and adapted to fly-fishing or swimming the worm for grayling. In the lower lengths the river is slow and deep, and more attractive to the bottom-fisher than the wielder of the fly rod. When the river is fairly high, and clearing after a spate, very good takes of coarse fish may be expected, provided that places are properly ground-baited overnight.

A short reach below Mr. Mountney's water is private, but just past the Wire Works we come to a well-stocked water. Nearly all the fishing in the Ambergate vicinity is in the hands of Mr. Alton, the Hurt Arms Hotel, close to the station. Permission is granted to visitors to the house.

Here the Amber joins the Derwent, and the lower part of this stream is also preserved by Mr. Alton. The Amber has its source on the moors above Darley, and, flowing south-west of Ashover, unites with a branch running by Clay Cross and Stretton. These combined brooks pursue a course through Alfreton down to Ambergate. The Amber breeds trout and coarse fish, and in parts affords moderate fly-fishing.

Mr. Alfred E. Coates, who has an intimate knowledge of the Derwent in this length, has kindly furnished me with some useful notes on the fishing above and below Ambergate. ' Immediately below the Wire Works Weir is the best length about here,' says Mr. Coates. ' It contains a few large trout and pike, many large chub, barbel, dace, and a fair lot of perch and roach.' Mr. J. Glossop, Ambergate, has the fishing from a few fields on both the Amber and Derwent, and would probably grant permission to fair and well-conducted anglers. Mr. Coates informs me that the river here is well fished in the summer by visitors from Derby, Ripley, Chesterfield, and elsewhere. In the winter, when the fishing is perhaps at its best, very few anglers frequent this water. The big chub here are somewhat coy. They are heavy fish, and it is worth some trouble to catch them. I surmise that systematic baiting, and the use of ox-pith for bait, would account for some of these fine chub in severe weather.

At the termination of the Hurt Arms length we come to the upper boundary of the Belper Angling Club preserve. This length has about five miles of water, extending from Ambergate through Belper to Milford. The most convenient stopping-place is Belper, a pleasant little town on the Midland Railway, on the outskirts of the Peak District.*

In this stretch there is very deep water, half a mile of the river having a depth of twenty-two feet. Some heavy fish swim in these deeps, and throughout the length the coarse-fishing is good.

* Hotel: Red Lion.   Inn: The Beehive (landlord member of angling club).

The fish are roach, perch, dace, chub, bream, pike, and trout. Barbel are fairly plentiful. Roach up to 1 pound 10 ounces, and perch up to $2\frac{3}{4}$ pounds, have been taken from this water, besides many big bream. Ground-baiting is, of course, essential to success.

There are some very fine trout here. The biggest trout, of which I have authentic record, weighed $6\frac{1}{2}$ pounds. Trout of 2 to 3 pounds are frequently captured, especially in the early part of the season. The method of fishing is with float-tackle, with worms or wasp-grub for bait. In February, 1905, three trout, averaging 2 pounds, were caught in an afternoon's fishing.

Perch-fishing is at its best in January and February. Dace are abundant, and they take the artificial fly during the summer.

The secretary of the Belper Club is Mr. John Lee, 21, Nottingham Road, Belper. Members are elected, and the season subscription is 10s. 6d. Visitors may obtain tickets at 1s. for the day.

The length below the Belper water, extending almost to Derby, is in the hands of the Duffield Angling Club. My query whether visiting fishermen can obtain tickets has not elicited a reply.

CHAPTER XVII

THE AMBER

I HAVE briefly referred to this stream in the last chapter, and I will now inform the visitor to this district where he may find fishing in the Amber. The trout of this river have to contend with coarse fish in the struggle for existence. They are, therefore, not so abundant as in the tributaries higher up the course of the Derwent. Still, there are good trout in the Amber, and the average may be set down at $\frac{1}{2}$ pound.

A considerable stretch of this stream is rented by the Ripley and District Angling Association, who have lately turned in about 200 two-year-old trout into the club water. The Amber length is from Ball Bridge up to Pentrich wire-mills, and as three miles have lately been added in Wingfield Park, making altogether a long preserve, there is plenty of available water for fly and bait fishing. Visiting anglers are made

welcome, and the charge for fishing is very
moderate. One shilling is the cost of a day ticket
for all the waters rented by the society.

The coal and iron industry in this part of the
country has led to the rapid growth of the town
of Ripley, which is conveniently situated for the
visiting fisherman. There is no scarcity of accommodation in Ripley, or, if the angler prefers
quietude, he may seek lodgings at Pentrich or
Ambergate. In spite of the near encroachment
of mines and ironworks, the valley of the Amber
is still secluded and rural, and in it will be found
some very charming reaches of the little stream.

The growth on the banks is somewhat dis-
advantageous for fly-fishing, but the Amber can
be fished with the fly by anyone accustomed to
cope with obstructions to casting. As many as
fifteen brace of trout have been taken in one day
from this river. But this is probably the record
catch, and the average take is very much less.
Three to four brace of trout may be caught by a
fairly persevering fly-fisherman, and it is probable
that the bait-fisher will add a fish or two to this
number. The trout are not diminutive

Besides the Amber, the Ripley Society has the
right of fishing in a large part of Butterley

Reservoir, a sheet of water within ten minutes' walk from Ripley, and close to Butterley Station. This pool is not overgrown, the banks being meadowland, sloping gently to the water. It contains pike, perch, roach, and carp. The pike-fishing is best in September and October, and live-baiting from a boat is the usual method. Two rods have taken 70 pounds of pike from the reservoir in a day's fishing. The boat-hire is 1s. a day.

Roach are abundant in Butterley Reservoir, and but little ground-baiting is necessary to bring the fish together. There is good bank fishing. The water is never quite clear in this pool. Some big carp have been caught here.

At Codnor Park the society has another reservoir, which also gives very fair baskets of coarse fish of several kinds. There is, therefore, variety in the fishing to be obtained in the neighbourhood of Ripley, while the Derwent at Ambergate and Belper is within a short railway ride.

Fishermen must observe the following rules of the Ripley Angling Association : Fair angling is only allowed, and not more than one rod is per-mitted to a ticket-holder. Pike under 18 inches, trout under 8 inches, and perch under 8 inches, must be returned to the water. Members of the association pay an entrance-fee of 5s., and a quarterly subscription of 1s., payable in advance. Visiting anglers can obtain day permits from Mr. George Slater, Secretary to the Angling Association, Ripley.

Fishermen are requested to avoid passing through standing corn and growing grass, and to close all gates by the riverside.

CHAPTER XVIII

DERBY AND AROUND

DERBY is a convenient point of approach to most of the fishing waters described in these pages. Visiting anglers from London and the South of England will pass through the town *en route* for the Derwent and its numerous tributaries, and should they wish to break their journey, they will find good hotel accommodation and a pleasant angling atmosphere in the old town. Derby has about fifty fishing clubs, and many miles of river and canal fishing are accessible by rail and road. In bygone days the Derwent was fishable close to the town, but with the spread of population, and the increase of sources of pollution, the times have changed, and anglers are now compelled to go further afield for their recreation.

The most influential angling society in Derby is that of the Midland Institute. All the members are in the employment of the Midland Railway

Company. Those who belong to the admirable Institute pay 7s. 6d. a year for membership of the Fishing Club, while non-members pay 10s. This strong association owns the fishing in many miles of the Trent and several canals, besides a considerable acreage of ponds. The rents of these waters amount to £100 a year, and the cost of preservation represents a still further sum.

Naturally, the Midland Institute Fishing Club desire to retain exclusive right over their own fishing lengths and pools. Visitors must, therefore, pay for the privilege of access to these waters, and the charge for 'outsiders' for the season is £2 2s. No short-period tickets are issued to strangers. The secretary is Mr. Bannister, Midland Railway Offices, Derby.

From all that I have seen and heard, I do not consider the cost of a season's fishing exorbitant. Some of the best coarse-fishing water in England is owned by the club. The perch and roach of the Trent are no mean fish, and the waters contain plenty of chub, bream, and pike. An evening's fishing in the Trent last summer yielded six roach, weighing 7 pounds ; and early in September, 1904, a brace of roach, scaling 3 pounds, were lured by the attraction of wheat. Very heavy catches of roach and bream are sometimes recorded from the club waters.

Certain canal reaches belonging to the Midland Institute Club can be fished by the public, on payment of 6d. a day.   These lengths are on the North Staffordshire Canal, the Derby Canal, and also on the Cromford Canal from Langley Mill to Cromford.   This stretch, which is amid very charming scenery in the neighbourhood of Whatstandwell, is thirteen miles long.   Here and there good bream are to be found in these canals, but the commonest fish are roach and gudgeon.   This canal is mostly shallow.

Anglers should venerate Derby, for there lived Herbert Spencer, one of the greatest thinkers and teachers of our age, and one of the keenest and most scientific of fishermen.   Derby is sadly deficient in the pride of venerating this illustrious son.   As a boy, Spencer spent most of his holiday time in fishing in the Derwent and the canals. He made his own ' hair tackles,' and exhibited, in his recreation of angling, the same ardour and originality that he displayed in philosophy and sociology.   In later years, Herbert Spencer became a salmon fisherman, and an enthusiast of sea-trout angling in Scotland.   But it was in the waters around Derby that he acquired rudimentary knowledge of the gentle craft.

From the Midland railway-station at Derby the visiting angler can reach over a score of fishing-places by short railway journeys. The whole lengths of the Derwent and Wye are easily accessible at almost any point from the Midland stations. Coarse-fishermen can travel hence to the best swims on the Trent and Dove, while the fly-fisher, bound for mid-waters of the Dove, can approach that river from Ashbourne viâ Derby, or visit the upper lengths of the Manifold and Dove from the charming town of Buxton.

Chellaston and Swarkestone Station, a rail-ride of ten minutes from Derby, is within one and a half miles of the Trent. Swarkestone is a pretty village on the riverside,* close to the handsome stone bridge. The Trent is here a fine wide stream, with deeps and scours and open banks for the greater part. It has many tempting swims for the bottom-fisher both above and below Swarkestone. Mr. R. Sale, Repton, near Derby, has the right over the length on the left bank.

Pike, perch, roach, chub, bream, dace, and a very few trout frequent this stretch. The dace

* Hotel: Crewe and Harpur Arms; several bedrooms.

rise to an artificial fly, and chub may be taken by the same means. Bream feed most readily in August. In half a day's fishing, to three rods, 20 pounds of roach, dace, and bream have been caught here. Fletcher, the water-bailiff, Barrow-on-Trent, Derby, provides live-bait, and will procure some large Trent gudgeon for anglers who give him a few days' notice.

Chellaston is also the station for a long canal length belonging to the Midland Institute Club. Tickets are issued at 6d. a day.

The Foremark Fishery, above Swarkestone, is in the hands of Mr. Newbold, The Elms, King's Newton, Derby, who issues season tickets at 21s. This is a well-stocked length of the Trent, and I am told that it gives good sport to roach, perch, and pike fishermen.

CHAPTER XIX

COMBS RESERVOIR FISHERY

THIS large sheet of water, which covers eighty acres, lies in a valley between Chapel-en-le-Frith and Whaley Bridge. The first-named town is situated among the heights of the Peak Country, twenty-three miles from Manchester. The Midland station at Chapel-en-le-Frith is within two miles from the reservoir. Close to the water is the quaint little inn, with the sign of the Hanging Gate, a house much frequented by fishermen throughout the year. Among the names of visitors to the inn, in the visitors' book, is that of Sir Henry Irving, who testifies to the kindness of the host.

On Sundays there is often a great gathering of anglers at Combs Reservoir, for the fishing is within a short railway journey from Sheffield and Manchester. There is beauty in the surroundings of this pool, and a fair number of fish in the water.

The reservoir is very deep in parts. In places it is said to be 50 feet deep, but the shores are shallow in most parts. One side of the pool is fringed with withes, which grow from the swamps bordering the water, and there are two or three arms which can only be fished from a boat. To reach the deeper water from the banks, a leger is useful, but many fishermen use float-tackle.

Some years ago the lake was private property, and at one time it contained a fine head of trout. Being well supplied with feeders from the hills, native trout from the brooks took up their quarters in the pool, and soon grew to the proportions of loch trout. In an evil hour pike made their appearance in the water, and it is hinted that they were introduced by a malicious person. Whatever may be the reason for the advent of the pike, it is a fact that the trout-fishing declined after the introduction or immigration of these fish of prey.

I am informed that a former proprietor once took 40 pounds of trout from the pool in a day's fishing. Nowadays the reservoir is stocked with coarse fish, though trout are not uncommon, and many have been turned in. Five hundred two-year-old trout were turned in lately, and they will no doubt give sport in coming seasons. If the pool was well stocked with trout, and the coarse fish greatly diminished in number, Combs Fishery would give very excellent sport to the fly-fisher, for it has all the features of a trout-lake. The secretary informs me that in 1902-1903, 1,800 trout were turned in, and in 1903-1904, 1,500. These were all two-year-old fish.

The reservoir is rented by the County Palatine Anglers' Association, one of the biggest of the Northern clubs. Mr. T. Driver, 44, Bury Street, Salford, is the secretary. Season tickets are issued at 5s. Day tickets cost 1s. Tickets are sold at the Hanging Gate Inn. The charge for boats for two persons is 1s. per day ; for three persons, 2s. 6d. ; for four persons, 3s. ; and tickets must be purchased by boat-hirers.

One rod and line is allowed to each angler, but an extra rod may be used for pike. The close season is from October 2 to February 1 for trout, and from November 15 to June 15 for coarse fish, except pike, which may be taken at any time. All fish under the following scale must be returned to the water immediately : Trout, 8 inches ; roach, 6 inches ; rudd, 6 inches ; bream, 8 inches ; tench, 7 inches ; perch, 6 inches. Pike and gudgeon may be taken any length. A large number of coarse fish have been turned in.

Perch have been caught up to 3 pounds in weight. Pike do not give the sport that might be expected, though there is reason to suppose that there are many in the water. Good trout are captured now and then by bottom-fishermen, and in the summer some sport might be obtained by fly-fishing or trolling the minnow from a boat. The water is well fished, especially on Sundays. Boat fishing might prove successful in some of the quieter and deeper parts of the reservoir, especially if places were baited overnight. There is sleeping accommodation at the inn, which is a few steps from the pool.

CHAPTER XX

GRAYLING FISHING IN DERBYSHIRE

I CONFESS that I grieve to hear of the disrepute into which the grayling appears to have fallen of late. Here is a game fish, say what you will, and one that will show sport long after the close of the trout season. He is handsome, bold, interesting, and intelligent, and knows well how to survive in the struggle for existence. In this matter the grayling seems to be more astute than his companion the brown trout. Grayling are prolific ; they replenish the waters rapidly—too rapidly from the point of view of certain trout preservers.

It is a vexed question. I fear that I have no new argument in defence of the grayling. One intelligent observer will inform you that these fish are as mischievous to trout as eels or chub ; other equally enlightened authorities absolve the grayling from the sin of ova-eating, and declare that trout eat the spawn of grayling with avidity. Who shall decide when pisciculturists disagree ? Is universal war to be waged on the grayling ? Is he really a ' vermin ' ?

There is something weird and inscrutable about grayling. Why do they increase quicker than trout ? Why do they show themselves almost everywhere in a river on some days, and keep entirely out of sight on other days ? Why do they avoid small tributaries and spawn in the main streams ? Why do they often rise twenty times to an artificial fly before deciding to swallow it ? Why are they one day coy and the next reckless in rising to a fly ? Verily, the grayling appears to me a more bewildering fish than the wily trout.

Cotton seems to have set the fashion of sneering at the grayling or umber. He calls him ' one of the deadest-hearted fishes in the world.' This is a libel. I have caught grayling in the Dee, Derwent, Dove, Wye, Manifold, Yore, and Tees, and had many a good fight with fish of a pound and less. Let us grant that a grayling has not quite the pluck and strength of a trout. He does not tear out your line from the reel in such furious rushes as those of a well-conditioned trout, nor does he often hurl himself three or four times from the water in his endeavours to escape from the hook. But he does undoubtedly show fight, and, what is more, he has the wit to free himself more frequently than the trout.

Even Cotton admitted that the umber is a pleasant fish on the table : ' For his flesh, even in his worst season, is so firm, and will so easily calve (*sic*) that in plain truth he is very good meat at all times ; but in his perfect season, which, by the way, none but an overgrown grayling will ever be, I think him so good a fish as to be little inferior to the best trout that I ever tasted in my life.' True, most excellent Piscator. And I would add that the sport-giving quality of the grayling is quite equal to his edible virtue. ' In my humble opinion,' says Edward Jesse, ' they are a much better fish than a trout.'

George Agar Hansard, in his book upon Welsh fishing, also lauds the gastronomic charm of *Salmo thymallus*. Izaak Walton, on the other hand, declared that the grayling is ' not so good to eat or to angle for ' as the trout. Mr. R. B. Marston, in his little work upon ' Walton and the Earlier Fishing Writers,' says of Cotton's statement about dead-hearted fish : ' I have killed a fair show of these beautiful fish in almost every grayling river of this country, and have often found them fight better than a trout, especially in the Test and the Costa.'   In the late autumn a 2-pound grayling, or even a pounder, will often contend with the angler quite as valiantly as a trout of those weights, and even more so, as Mr. Marston testifies.

There is little doubt that grayling exhibit a truly marvellous fecundity in the length of the Wye between Bakewell and Rowsley. Netting out seems only to check the increase, and it would probably be an impossible matter to banish the grayling from this productive stream.   In the Upper Dove I am fairly well assured that the grayling threaten to outnumber the trout, and it is an undoubted fact that they are more abundant than trout in the Rocester and Uttoxeter stretches of that river.

The Manifold teems with grayling, and I should say that they are bigger, on an average, in this stream than in the Derwent.   From Ashopton down to Belper there are hosts of grayling in the Derwent, and I believe that in certain reaches they are more numerous than trout.   The Derbyshire rivers have, therefore, special claim upon grayling anglers.

The effects of education upon the Derbyshire grayling are not so marked as upon the trout of this county. Notwithstanding, the grayling of the Wye are very far from unacquainted with the wiles of fishermen. They are much warier than the grayling of the Welsh Dee and the Yore. The grayling of Derbyshire also differ somewhat in their habits from the grayling of Wales and Yorkshire. I doubt whether our grayling could be enticed from the Wye, in any numbers, by the method of float-fishing pursued in Yorkshire. Rocester, on the Dove, seems to be the only place where bait-fishing for Derbyshire grayling is followed in the Yorkshire style. I have never seen a Derbyshire angler wade into the Derwent during a hard frost in January, and ' swim the worm ' with float-tackle, as anglers do in the Yore in midwinter. This is not saying that there is no winter bait-fishing for grayling in the Derbyshire rivers. But few anglers, if any, work in the Yorkshire style.

I have not often tried the worm or maggot for grayling in Derbyshire. My few essays in this direction have been made in the mid-reaches of the Derwent, and I have not captured many fish. But I have seen other fishermen rewarded with good catches from October till Christmas, and especially during sharp weather. Elsewhere in these pages I have described the favourite winter and summer haunts of grayling, and I refer the reader to the index.

Grayling probably spawn in April. Unfortunately, as far as my experience serves, that is just the time when they are inclined to take the wet fly in the Wye, Dove, and Manifold; so that a day's excursion may result in the capture of grayling at the very season when their attentions are least welcome.

About the end of June grayling begin to haunt the pools, and to lurk near the surface. The tails of pools are their favoured positions when flies are about. They rise voraciously on certain days, as I have pointed out, and appear to put down the trout.

Derbyshire grayling will almost jostle one another to snatch at the iron-blue dun on cool days in the early summer; and later on they take the olive dun with extreme avidity. Last year on the Dove I noted that on one day, in the height of the Mayfly time, the grayling seized upon every green drake that appeared on the water, while the trout scornfully rejected these tasty flies, and stubbornly regaled themselves on the tiniest of black midges.

All kinds of wonderful artificial flies are used by Derbyshire grayling anglers. I have nothing to say against any of these lures. My own experience is that grayling, when feeding on the surface, prefer the natural fly that is in evidence. Still, far be it from me to lay down any hard-and-fast rule upon the use of flies. Last June a friend of mine caught a grayling of $1\frac{1}{2}$ pounds, with a coch-y-bonddu—a fly never seen in the natural state upon Derbyshire rivers ; and I know another angler who finds this fly attractive to the grayling of Dovedale. I have caught grayling with at least a score of different flies, and I have no favourite. But the apple-green, the fiery bumble, the golden earwig, and other local patterns should be carried by the fisherman.

Grayling appear to find attraction in gaudily-dressed flies with tinsel bodies. Green is a colour that they appreciate, but they will often exhibit a preference for sober-coloured flies. I think that in winter fishing, especially with the sunk fly, the lure should be fairly bright. Such flies are used in Dovedale during October and November.

Franck, an old angling writer, confesses great

faith in natural flies and grubs as baits for grayling. ' But of all natural insects which accommo-
date the art,' says this quaint writer, ' the green
drake is that sovereign ophthalmic that opens his
eyes, and shuts them again, with the hazard of
his life, and the loss of his element.   Yet for this
fly admirer there is another bait, and that is the
munket, or a sea-green grub, generated, as I take
it, amongst owlder trees.   The like product issues
from the willows, so does it from the sallow ; nor
is the primp force denied this vegetable animal,
save only they are different in splendour and
colour, as also as different in shape and proportion.'

I cannot identify that fearsome creature, ' the
munket of the owlder trees,' but I assume that it
is a species of caterpillar highly relished by the
umber or grayling.   Green is certainly a hue that
attracts grayling, and the green grasshopper is
therefore a very good bait for thymallus.   Walton
also notes the fondness of the grayling for lively
colours.   From his ' Observations of the Umber
or Grayling,' it would seem that this fish was not
very highly esteemed by the author of ' The
Complete Angler.'

In the Welsh grayling streams I have noticed

that this fish is not so disposed to take the fly in frosty as in mild weather during the autumn. I remember an excellent rise of grayling to duns, in the Dee, on a mild Christmas Day. Frost is said to sharpen the appetite of grayling, and I believe that is a fairly established fact; but I think that bait-fishing is the method for hard weather.

Grayling have a tantalizing habit of flashing up to a floating fly, taking a quick pluck at it, and expelling it instantly from their mouths. Small grayling of $\frac{1}{4}$ pound will play this trick again and again. I have often taken fish that must have felt the hook several times, for a pricked grayling does not appear to be greatly perturbed. It is curious, too, how confiding grayling often prove to be when the angler is wading up-stream. They will rise under the very point of the rod, if the water is not much disturbed. It is, therefore, as a rule, easier to stalk a grayling than a trout.

In some rivers shoals of little grayling, scarcely bigger than minnows, congregate in certain parts, and rise five or six at a time to an artificial fly. I have not been much troubled in this way in the Derbyshire streams, though I cannot account for the reason. In the Upper Dove one day I cer-

tainly noted an immense number of diminutive
grayling on the feed, and I have seen a rise of these
fingerlings in the Wye. But the grayling that rise
most freely in these waters are fish of a presentable
size.

After the spawning season grayling resort to
every part of the rivers. You are as likely to take
them in the trout runs as in the pools ; but I
believe that the biggest grayling prefer the pools
and long stills during the summer and autumn.
They often lie quite close to the banks, especially
under the boughs of alders, where, no doubt, they
await the ' munket ' and other grubs that drop
from the trees. The extreme end of long, fairly
deep shallows, such as are frequently found in the
course of the Derwent above Whatstandwell and
in Darley Dale, are parts that should be watched
by the grayling fisherman in summer and autumn.
In the deeper pools of the Wye, especially in
eddies, grayling gather in large numbers when
flies are coming down the river.

Persistency is one of the secrets of success in
fly-fishing for grayling. You need never fear that
feeding grayling will retire disgusted with your
attentions. They will come up again, if you give
them a few minutes' rest, and the thirtieth cast

may take the biggest fish in the pool, after he has repeatedly rejected your ash dun or claret bumble. Amid a hatch of natural flies, you will often obtain a rise to every cast of your fly, but you may only capture a brace of fish from that spot in the end.

Only in certain lengths of the Derwent is bait-fishing for grayling commonly practised during the autumn and winter months. Bait is prohibited in Dovedale, in the Wye, and private lengths generally, but the worm and maggot may be used in the Dove at Rocester. Derwent bait-fishermen sometimes use ordinary roach-floats and fine tackle, and fish from the bank, remaining stationary in one place for some time. This is a different method from the ranging and wading adopted in other parts of the kingdom. In severe weather the red worm is the best bait in the Derwent, and under milder conditions gentles may be used. A few worms or gentles are thrown into the top of a run before the fisherman swims his bait down.

October is considered the best month of the year for grayling fishing in Derbyshire, though the fish are usually in condition, and begin to rise well, in August. The artificial fly will take grayling up to Christmas, but, as a rule, these rivers do not fish well with the fly after November. In January there is not a great chance of making a basket with the fly, though it is often a favourable month for the bait fisherman. During hot weather grayling frequently rise freely at dusk, but as soon as darkness sets in they appear to leave the surface of the pools, and to give place to those trout of the warier order, which feed chiefly at night.

That grayling enjoy a touch of north wind during the summer is shown by experience. When trout are ' off ' upon cool days in July or August, grayling are often hungry, and on the quest for surface food. A change of wind will often bring grayling on the feed. They will rise greedily at times when snow or hail are falling, and especially in intervals of sunshine between such showers. Snow-broth in the streams does not affect them if the temperature sinks below the freezing-point.

Grayling of 1 pound are fairly common in the Derbyshire waters, and heavier fish are taken every season. The fish of ½ pound and upwards give good sport, and rise with boldness upon favourable days. Whether you seek to entice the umber with the sunk fly, dry fly, natural fly, or red worm, you will find him responsive in the rivers of Derbyshire.

> 'Umber or grayling in the streams he'll lie,
> Hovering his fins at every silly fly ;
> Fond of a feather, you shall see him rise
> At emmets, insects, hackles, drakes, and flies.'

I shall be sorry to hear of the doom of this sport-giving fish.   Will not one of our scientific fish culturists determine, once and for all, whether the umber deserves the evil character that has been attached to him ?   Since the days of Walton the grayling has kept company with the trout in the rivers of Derbyshire, and the trout are certainly not on the point of extinction.   It is pleasant to vary one's fishing from trout to grayling as the seasons come round.

CHAPTER XXI

HINTS UPON FISHING IN DAMS AND POOLS

THE term ' dam ' is generally applied in Derby-shire and the adjoining counties to any sheet of still water, whether or no it is connected with a mill. Thus reservoirs, constructed for supplying water to the towns, are usually called dams, and the same word is used to describe a still pool on a river. Some of the dams in the district have been designed for the purpose of affording water-power to mills, and in such cases small streams have been widened out and deepened to form a series of pools. In other instances, as on the Lathkill and Bradford streams, dams have been artificially constructed in order to convert a sluggish water into alternate pools and runs suitable for fly-fishing.

The straight, the horseshoe, and the half-weirs on some of the private lengths of the Derbyshire trout-streams are ingenious contrivances for improving the water, and providing those sharp, broken runs that trout love. The Dove, for example, in Narrow Dale, has been made into an excellent stretch of fly-fishing water by the system of damming. At Chatsworth the Derwent affords another instance of the utility of dam-making in slow and unbroken reaches of a river. A very elaborate series of weirs may be seen on the Lathkill, where Art has aided Nature in the interest of the fly-fisherman.

As these pools, which often abound with big trout, are hardly comparable with any other kind of water in the kingdom, I propose to give a few words of counsel upon the most profitable mode of fishing in them. A Derbyshire dam is not like the pool of a Yorkshire or Welsh river. Except in high floods, there is scarcely a perceptible current through some of these dams, and, moreover, they are usually quite clear, the bottom of the river being visible in 6 or 7 feet of water.

Now, a casual inspection of one of these pools on a hot, bright day in June would lead the inexperienced visitor to suppose that fly-fishing in such translucent and dead water is next to useless, and it is probable that he would pass on to the next run. And yet how enticing are these pools when a good hatch of fly brings the trout up to the surface, and the water is ringed here and there with rises. You may see trout of a pound and heavier quietly ' standing ' in all parts of the water, awaiting the alders or ash duns that come tripping along with fairy feet. Undoubtedly this is a rise that one does not care to pass by ; but the difficulty is to stalk up to within casting distance of this all too visible trout, and to throw a dry fly without putting down half the fish in the dam.

The circumvention of the goodly-proportioned trout of these river dams is certainly no easy matter. But it is a most fascinating pastime to try one's skill against these wary fish. The chances are that no favouring wind disturbs the surface of the water in ripples, for this dam is sheltered by wooded heights and cliffs of limestone. Now and then an up-stream breeze, gaining strength in the gully, sweeps across the pool, and troubles the water for a brief half-hour. Yet all too soon it subsides, and in the dead calm, the fisherman sits down in despair to smoke a pipe, and to covet those lovely trout that constantly break the surface just off that fringe of willow-herb and meadow-sweet. Watch that red-and-golden fellow, how he placidly sucks in the little

pale duns that pass over his snout.   He is at least
$1\frac{1}{2}$ pounds in weight, and in the very pink of
condition and beauty.   What a fight he would give
on this little 9-feet rod and that finely-tapered cast!

And here, in this corner, where the beech-tree
droops to the water, you may see at least a dozen
plump trout, poised on the look-out for insects
that drop from the boughs.   What a tempting
spectacle !   Yet you dare not approach them, for
no sooner does your shadow touch the water in
their vicinity than the whole dozen sink down out
of sight.   Ten to one are the chances of success,
if you could only drop a blue-bottle over their
noses.   But the sun is behind you, and it is well-
nigh impossible to pass your rod through the
branches of that beech-tree.

' It is no good !' murmurs the visiting angler,
as he turns away from the dam.   ' If I dare to cast,
I scare every fish in the place.'   Quite so, my
friend ; I have known the same trial.   But, believe
me, the case is not hopeless.   What do you say
to a brace of pounders from this still, transparent
water ?   Impossible ?   No, I have done it, and
I will do it again, please the Fates.   Have patience,
and listen for awhile.

There are four ways of getting on terms with

those big trout in the dam.   One of them I do not consider legitimate in this water, and that is waiting for a flood, and fishing with worm-tackle and a float.   I only mention this plan to bar it, for it would be a sin to haul out those noble fish on bottom tackle.   If you will have patience, I will promise you finer sport than that.   The second method is fishing with a live fly, which I consider to be permissible under certain restrictions.   For example, the day is glittering, and you have tried the artificial fly in vain ; and yet the trout are taking anything that comes along, and enjoying a feast of surface insects.   Do not imagine, however, that it is child's play to fish with a natural fly in such water.   It is by no means easy.   First of all, there is very little cover around the pool. Moreover, having put your live fly on the hook, it is extremely difficult to keep it there until such time as you drop it gently in the swirl of a rise. To reach that pertinacious trout by the little patch of arrow-head, you will have to cast your natural fly.

To succeed in this sort of fishing, one must be systematic.   Provide a small butterfly-net and a tin box for your flies.   Pull out about a dozen yards of your reel-line, and rub it well with vaseline.   Treat your fine-drawn cast in like manner, and attach a small bronzed hook. If the day is dull, you will find flies of various sorts reposing upon the reeds and nettles.*   Alders, drakes, daddy-long-legs, house-flies, blue-bottles, and small beetles should be promptly secured at sight.   Place your fly on the hook without injuring him, which is, of course, easier said than done. Try to transfix him through the least vital part of his body. Remember that this is not dapping. It is *casting* with a live fly.

I maintain that this is the most difficult kind of angling extant. It is at least three times as intricate and worrying as dry-fly fishing against a stiff breeze. But, for all that, casting the dry fly on still water is a mighty interesting sport when big trout are the object of your patient cunning. Nothing can be prettier in the whole art of fishing than this process of casting your live fly over a trout in 2 feet of bright water, and seeing the wily victim take it with a splash. A trout rarely rises to a dry fly in this hearty, jubilant fashion. But this is the real thing, the very fly that he is taking, wing for wing, and leg for leg.   He takes it with a dash and a swirl, with no hint of hesitancy. Always ? No, not quite always. You

* Insects are usually on the wing upon bright days.

may have crushed and mutilated your fly in putting it on the hook. You may easily drown your fly, especially in making a long cast, and a drowned natural fly is worse than useless. Again, you may thrash the water with your reel-line in your anxiety to reach your fish.

These and other mishaps will inevitably add variety to this mode of dam-fishing. Nevertheless, if you persevere, I promise that you will meet with your reward in the capture of some of the biggest trout in that dam. I have caught trout by this means up to $1\frac{1}{2}$ pounds in weight upon days when they would not look at a dry fly, let it be presented ever so lightly in the circle of their rises. Success in this kind of fishing depends upon several essentials. You must look as much unlike a man as possible. Crawl, grope, wriggle, emulate the snake, adopt any method of locomotion other than upright, straightforward walking. You have to get that fly alive over your fish before he can see you or your waving rod. Set your teeth, and swear that you will accomplish this stalk, and after some failures you will learn the knack of effacing yourself and keeping the fly on the hook.

There is nothing more absolutely irresistible to

a big trout on the feed than a live insect.   And, as
I have said, there is nothing more difficult than to
get that fly to him alive and in a natural manner.
Your fly must drop and flutter.   If it flops and
remains motionless, send a tiny shudder from the
wrist along your rod, and let it be no more than a
shudder.   By this ruse you may convey a sem-
blance of life to your expiring fly.   Dapping is
a boy's game compared with casting a live fly on
calm water.

We will suppose that a breeze has found its way
to the sheltered pool, and that no trout appear to
be rising.   The wind is cool, and there are very
few flies visible.   Take a Wickham's Fancy or a
March brown, with a little gold twist to the body,
and fix it to a fine cast.   Stalk up to the bank,
and kneel down.   Before you is a nice patch of
rippled water.   Throw into it, let your fly sink,
and work it slowly under water.   In May and
June, in dull, windy weather, I have often taken
from two to three brace of dam trout by wet-fly
fishing.   At dusk the wet fly is often taken almost
fiercely by trout that have been sluggish throughout the day.   If you have leave to fish after dark,
which is against the rules in most club waters, you
may use a rather bigger fly, with a tinsel body.

Foster's ' woolly bear ' may be often used with success in dam fishing.

Wet-fly fishing in the Derbyshire dams is not like loch-fishing, because, as I have said, the pools are usually in sheltered dales. Upon a loch you have the advantage of a large sheet of water, well searched by the wind. Here you have only an acre or less of water, which the wind rarely ruffles into billows. For these reasons wet-fly fishing often fails in dams. Still, as I have said, there are occasions when a sunk fly will bring several good trout to the creel. After a spate, for instance, when the water is tinted, there is a fair chance for the wet-fly angler, and also upon days of exceptional storm and wind. In the Tansley Dams, near Matlock, the wet fly is, to my mind, more effective than the floating fly.

Dry-fly fishing in dams and pools without a stream is quite possible. It is, indeed, a far more successful method of lake-fishing than most anglers imagine. Hitherto most dry-fly fishermen have insisted that this form of fishing can only be practised upon moving water. This is a mistake. You can catch trout with a floating fly in any sort of water except very turbulent streams. The slightest breath of wind on a dam gives a lifelike motion to your fly, and deceives trout. I have proved this over and over again. Besides, it is possible to give such a gentle twitch to your fly that no drag is perceptible. When trout are rising in still pools, very careful stalking is necessary, and your fly must not be cast recklessly into any rings that you may see. Mark a fish that means business, one that steadily snaps up every fly that passes near to him, and try him with an imitation of the natural insect. If a favouring puff of wind bears your oiled fly near his range of vision, it is almost certain that a feeding trout will at least rise to it.

In a dam which I often fish with the dry fly there is no current whatever in the height of summer. The water most frequented by trout is not more than a foot deep, and is much shallower near the bank. I have marked trout here in water so shallow that their back fins were almost in the air, and yet, strange as it may appear, these trout will often take a dry fly with eagerness. But all is lost if one of them catch sight of the angler. At this place there is a capital natural screen of tall nettles. My face and hands are so often stung while landing trout here that by the end of the summer I am quite inoculated to nettle-stings.

I will now reveal a lure which has often served me well in dam-fishing. This is the imitation coch-y-bonddu made by Mr. Kennedy, Solihull, Warwickshire. I have praised this beetle elsewhere, and I do so here because it does what its inventor claims for it. This insect, which Mr. Kennedy has so well imitated, is called the fern-web in Devonshire, and the bracken-clock in the North. I have never seen the natural insect in Derbyshire, yet upon dams it is a very good lure. The little beetle floats right side up, no matter how you cast it ; and even when trout refuse it, they rarely fail to come up for a look at the strange beast. The floating coch-y-bonddu can be cast like a fly. It will float better if the cast is greased, but I do not always trouble to vaseline my cast when fishing with this beetle. I consider the use of the coch-y-bonddu to be quite as legitimate as the use of the dry fly ; indeed, it is just as artistic to fish with this counterfeit as with an ash dun. On slow streams the coch-y-bonddu beetle should be cast like a dry fly, and allowed to float down to a rising fish. To avoid damaging the beetle when extracting it from a fish's mouth, it is well to use the bone disgorger which is supplied with each of the baits.

Fishing for trout in the large reservoirs of the North Midlands may be likened to lake-fishing in Scotland or Wales. The wet fly is usually employed, and some anglers have two or three flies on their cast. A breeze is necessary for this sort of fishing, and on calm days fair success may attend the use of the dry fly, if the angler can watch the fly upon the water, and avoid showing himself to the trout.

Big trout in pools are often shy of the shallow water until dusk, when they come inshore to search for small fry, or flies that flutter from the banks. The bottom-fisher stands the best chance of taking one or two large fish during the daytime, provided that he can throw his bait into the deep water. This is practicable by using a leger tackle and a free-running reel ; but the leger in still water is not always so deadly as float-tackle. It is not easy to swing out a light quill or cork float, especially against the wind. Northern bottom-fishermen sometimes employ an ingenious plan for getting their worm or wasp-grub well out from the bank, though I do not know whether the method has been tried in this district.

Instead of a cork float, use a small medicine-phial, round in shape, and about three parts filled with water, and well corked.   This glass float can be fastened to the line with elastic bands, and adjusted to the proper depth.   The bait should swim clear of the bottom, and may even be in mid-water.   With such a float you can cast twice as far as with a cork or quill.   I am not a devotee of bait-fishing for trout, but in certain waters it is next to impossible to lure big trout with the fly, and the humble angler, who has no opportunity for learning the use of the fly-rod, naturally wishes to enjoy his sport upon his infrequent holidays. Gentles, wasp-grub, dock-grub, and worms of various kinds are good baits for the big trout of reservoirs.

In dams or pools with weedy bottoms, it should be your endeavour to keep a hooked trout as near the surface as possible.   If he dives down into the submerged jungle, it is a twenty-to-one chance that you will lose him, though by giving slack line and waiting for your fish to shift from his harbour you may sometimes outwit his desperate tactics for obtaining liberty.   With care and firmness, you may often rush a big trout along the surface of a weedy pool and into the net before he can quite make up his mind concerning his course of action.

I have never tried the blow-line on the Derbyshire dams and reservoirs.   Life is too short and
leisure too scant to achieve all that one desires in
the piscatorial art.   But why should not the blow-
line method succeed on the Damflask and other
pools of the Peak Country ?   It is well worth a
trial in June, when flies are fairly abundant over
the water.   I fancy that this mode of fishing
might have good results on breezy days at the
proper season of the year ; for, as I have said,
there is no more tempting bait for a lake trout
than a live fly skilfully presented during a rise.

I know one or two fishermen who appear to
disdain fly-fishing for trout in still water.   Now,
if it is a question of skill, I will assert that such
angling is quite as difficult as fishing in rivers.
It is, to my mind, a triumph to take a big trout
from a dam on a bright, calm day, whether the
means be wet, dry, or live fly-fishing.   If you
neglect the dams, you will certainly lose the
chance of trying terms with some of the heaviest
trout that swim in Derbyshire waters.   Try
your dry fly on a calm day in June or July,
and tell me whether this fishing does not
require even more skill and delicacy than casting
in moving water.

APPENDICES

I.

DISTRIBUTORS OF LICENSES UNDER THE TRENT CONSERVANCY, 1904.

AMBERGATE	..	W. Alton, Hurt Arms.
ASHBOURNE	..	⎰D. and W. H. Foster. ⎱Mrs. Grindey, Dovedale Hotel, Dovedale.
BAKEWELL	..	⎰T. Tyack, Rutland Arms Hotel. ⎱J. Carrington, Bridge Street.
BASLOW ..	..	J. Eades, Peacock Hotel.
BELPER ..	..	John Lee, Nottingham Road.
BUXTON ..	..	John Banks, Spring Gardens.
CHESTERFIELD	..	James Armistead, 16, Knifesmith Gate.
CROMFORD	..	S. C. Cooper, Greyhound Hotel.
DERBY ..	..	⎧S. Thomson, 15½, Friargate. ⎪J. Hinton, East Street. ⎨J. H. Saxton, London Road. ⎩C. K. Eddowes, 2, The Strand.
DOVEDALE	..	W. Evans, Izaak Walton Hotel.
DUFFIELD	..	E. Barnes, Railway Terrace.
ETWALL ..	..	W. Argyle.
HARTINGTON	..	J. E. Fosbrooke.
HATHERSAGE	..	Mrs. Ibbotson, Post Office.
HOPE ..	..	Geo. Ashton, Junior.
LONGNOR	..	Mrs. Gould, Crewe and Harpur Arms.

LEEK	Blakemore and Chell, 3, Sheep-market.
MILLER'S DALE..	T. R. Holmes.
MATLOCK BATH..	W. J. Hackney, South Parade.
MATLOCK BRIDGE	H. G. Hartley, Crown Square.
NOTTINGHAM ..	{ C. Jackson, 11, Drury Hill. E. West, 28, Sussex Street. J. Theaker, 2, Broad Marsh.
ROWSLEY ..	Miss S. Cooper, Peacock Hotel.
ROCESTER ..	T. Titley, Post Office.
SHEFFIELD ..	G. Wood, 117, Pinstone Street.
UTTOXETER ..	J. Stanley, Carter Street.
WIRKSWORTH ..	Mrs. Allen, Post Office.

II.

TACKLE MAKERS, FLY DRESSERS, ETC

ASHBOURNE ..	Messrs. Foster Bros., Midland Works. Steel-ribbed rods and special floating flies for the district.
BUXTON	J. Banks, Spring Gardens. General tackle.
DERBY	J. Hinton, East Street. Coarse-fishing tackle and bait.
DOVEDALE ..	W. Evans, Izaak Walton Hotel Flies for the Dove.
HARTINGTON ..	John Fosbrooke. Fly-tier.
MATLOCK ..	J. G. Eaton. Fly-tier for Derwent.
NOTTINGHAM ..	C Jackson, 11, Drury Hill. All angling accessories and baits.
SHEFFIELD ..	Messrs. Geo. Wood and Co., 117, Pinstow Street. Every class of rods. Flies for local dams and Derbyshire and Yorkshire rivers.

NEAREST STATION TO WATERS.

WATER.	STATION.	RAILWAY COMPANY.
AMBER ..	Ambergate, Butterley, Ripley	Midland
BUTTERLEY RESERVOIR..	Butterley	"
CHURNET ..	Rocester, Uttoxeter	North Staffordshire
COMB'S RESERVOIR	Chapel-en-le-Frith	Midland
DAMFLASK RESERVOIR	Sheffield	"
DERWENT, UPPER	Banford, Grindleford	"
" MID ..	Bakewell, Rowsley, Darley Dale, Matlock, Cromford	"
" LOWER	Whatstandwell, Belper, Duffield, Derby	"
DOVE, UPPER	Buxton	L. & N. W.
" MID	Hurdlow	"
" MID	Alsop-en-le-Dale, Thorpe	"
" LOWER	Ashbourne	L. & N. W. and Midland
LATHKILL ..	Rocester, Uttoxeter	North Staffordshire
	Rowsley, Bakewell	Midland
MANIFOLD, UPPER	Buxton	L. & N. W.
" LOWER	Hartington, Thorpe	"
" "	Ashbourne	Midland
RUDYARD LAKE..	Rudyard	North Staffordshire
TRENT (open waters)	Chellaston, Weston-on-Trent, Nottingham, Burton Joyce, Thurgarton, Fiskerton	Midland

INDEX

THE END

BILLING AND SONS, LTD., PRINTERS, GUILDFORD

BIBLIOLIFE

Old Books Deserve a New Life
www.bibliolife.com

Did you know that you can get most of our titles in our trademark **EasyScript**™ print format? **EasyScript**™ provides readers with a larger than average typeface, for a reading experience that's easier on the eyes.

Did you know that we have an ever-growing collection of books in many languages?

Order online:
www.bibliolife.com/store

Or to exclusively browse our **EasyScript**™ collection:
www.bibliogrande.com

At BiblioLife, we aim to make knowledge more accessible by making thousands of titles available to you – quickly and affordably.

Contact us:
BiblioLife
PO Box 21206
Charleston, SC 29413

Printed in Great Britain
by Amazon.co.uk, Ltd.,
Marston Gate.